The Power® Of:
Financial Calculations
for
1-2-3™

by

Robert E. Williams

Management Information Source, Inc.

Copyright 1983 by Management Information Source, Inc.
3543 N.E. Broadway, Portland, Oregon 97232
(503) 287-1462

First Printing

ISBN 0-943518-10-5

One of a series of instructional manuals on the use and application of computer programs.

1-2-3 is a trademark of Lotus Development Corporation
Cambridge, Mass.
(617) 492-7171

The Power Of:® is a registered trademark of Management Information Source, Inc.

Edited by: Estelle Phillips

PREFACE

The Power Of: Financial Calculations for 1-2-3 presents practical solutions to everyday problems facing the businessman. The purpose of these chapters is to aid in the many decision-making situations that face business people daily.

The emphasis in The Power Of: Financial Calculations for 1-2-3 is on presenting the solutions to real-life problems, rather than concentrating on explanations of theories and formulas.

For clarity in understanding where formulas are to be entered, the formula(s) in each exercise is displayed in an adjacent area in a box with an arrow pointing to the coordinate into which the formula is to be entered.

No special training is needed to benefit from this book. All the instructions are in plain English. The procedures necessary to perform each exercise are given to the reader in a step-by-step manner.

The Power Of: Financial Calculations for 1-2-3 will become your most valuable reference book in solving financial problems.

IF YOU OWN, OR ARE THINKING OF OWNING, 1-2-3, YOU SHOULD OWN THIS BOOK!

INTRODUCTION

The exercises in this book have been purposely designed to provide an opportunity to easily follow the logic of 1-2-3 functions, and then apply those functions to specific problems. It is important to note that the problems in the exercises have been specifically selected to demonstrate 1-2-3, as opposed to illustrating specific problem-solving methods.

Each exercise in The Power Of: Financial Calculations 1-2-3 is self-contained. Each demonstrates some special ability or abilities that will broaden your knowledge and skills in using 1-2-3 as a problem-solving tool for your special applications.

The 1-2-3 format is arranged on the computer screen in columns and rows. The 1-2-3 worksheet format is illustrated in Figure 1 with a grid superimposed on it to offer a visual concept for the following explanation.
The 1-2-3 worksheet columns are identified by letter designations, the rows by numbers. Each position where a column and row interesect is a ''coordinate'' location. Visualizing your worksheet as a street map, you can locate any coordinate on your worksheet using a letter and a number designation (such as B4) to identify its distinctive column and row intersection.

The relationships between values in coordinates on your worksheet are determined by simple instructions entered into the coordinates in the form of algebraic formulas. (Don't get panicky; that just means (a + b) and other similar expressions.) By visualizing the street map grid image and following the exercises, you will easily and quickly catch on to the powwer of 1-2-3 and how it can work for you.

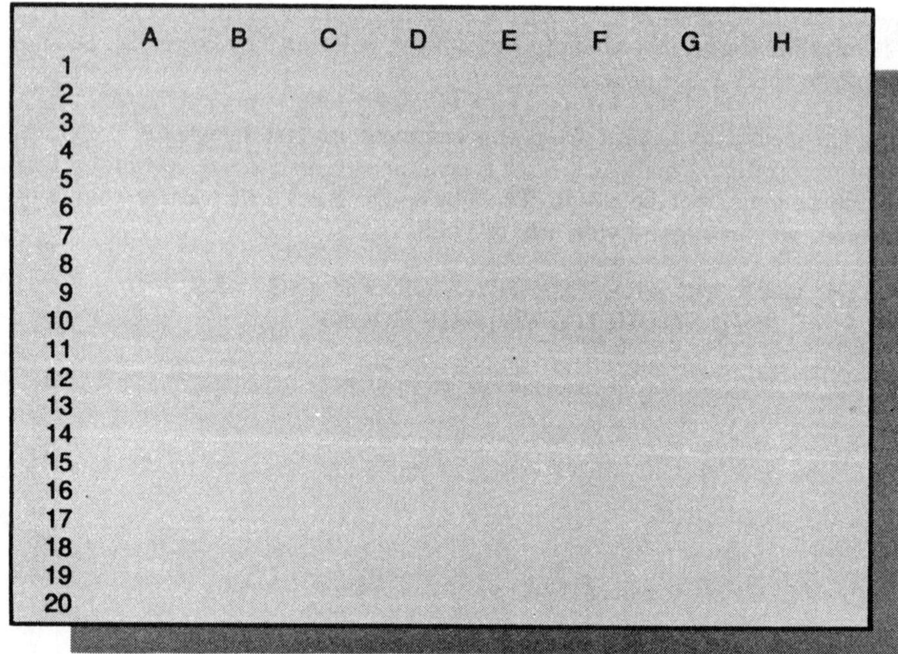

Figure 1

TABLE OF CONTENTS

CHAPTER ONE

FINANCING AND PURCHASING A HOME

DESCRIPTION

When considering the purchasing and financing of a home, several factors need to be considered: The minimum loan payment and maximum loan payment (min. loan payment plus tax and insurance, if applicable), the amount of the loan, the total purchase price and the down payment required.

In determining these factors, it will be necessary to know the buyer's gross monthly income, and what percent of his gross income the lending institution will allow him to apply to the monthly mortgage payment. It is necessary to also determine the annual interest rate, the number of compounding periods per year, the term (years) of the loan, the percent of down payment and the percent of tax and insurance required.

EXAMPLE

A prospective buyer of a home has a monthly income of $2700 and the bank requires that he apply 25% of that to his monthly mortgage payment. The interest rate is 12%, the number of compounding periods is 12, the term is 30 years. The bank also requires that a down payment of 15% be applied. The tax and insurance is 30%.

The buyer needs to know what his minimum loan payment, and also what his maximum loan payment would be. He also wants to know how large a loan amount he can afford, which will determine how much he can pay for a house (purchase price), and how much he would have to apply as a down payment on the house.

SETTING UP YOUR WORKSHEET - ENTERING LABELS

USE THE FOLLOWING STEP-BY-STEP DIRECTIONS FOR ENTERING THE LABELS IN FIGURE 1:

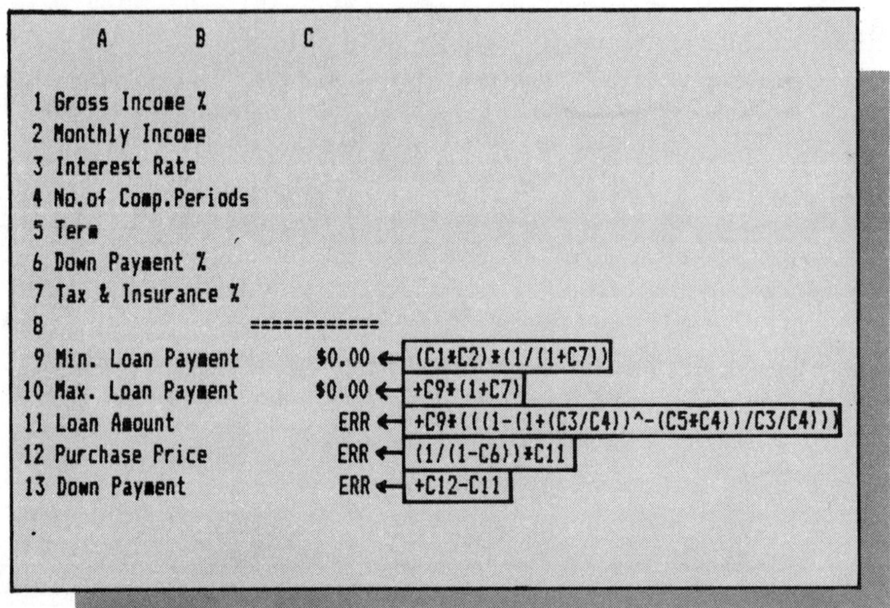

Figure 1

First, column C needs to be expanded to allow for 12 characters.

Place your cursor on column C and type:

/W	starts WORKSHEET command
C	selects Column-Width option
S	selects Set option
12	number of spaces in column
RETURN	executes the command

Now enter your labels, starting in A1 and continuing through A13, exactly as illustrated in Figure 1, retaining exact row and column locations of all information.

Next enter the double-dashed line in row 8,

Place your cursor on C8 and type:

\	starts REPEAT command
=	equal sign, label to be repeated
RETURN	executes the command

Now that you have entered your labels and the double-dashed line, you will begin entering the formulas which will calculate the unknown values.

ENTERING FORMULAS

USE THE FOLLOWING STEP-BY-STEP DIRECTIONS FOR ENTERING THE FORMULAS WHICH WILL CALCULATE THE UNKNOWN VALUES.

Formula one, to the right of Min. Loan Payment, calculates the minimum loan payment, using the following information: percent of gross income, monthly gross income and the tax and insurance percentage.

Place your cursor on C9 and type:

(C 1 * C 2) * (1 / (1 + C 7))	formula
RETURN	enters the formula

Formula two, to the right of Max. Loan Payment, calculates the maximum loan payment, which is the minimum loan payment plus tax and insurance.

Place your cursor on C10 and type:

+ C 9 * (1 + C 7)	formula
RETURN	enters the formula

Formula three, to the right of Loan Amount, calculates the amount of the loan.

Place your cursor on C11 and type:

+ C 9 * (((1 — (1 + (C 3 / C 4))ˆ — (C 5 * C 4)) / (C 3 / C 4)))	formula
RETURN	enters the formula

Formula four, to the right of Purchase Price, calculates the total purchase price.

Place your cursor on C12 and type:

(1 / (1 — C 6)) * C 1 1	formula
RETURN	enters the formula

Formula five, to the right of Down Payment, determines the amount of down payment.

Place your cursor on C13 and type:

+ C 1 2 — C 1 1   formula

RETURN   enters the formula

Now you will format the coordinates into which you have just entered the formulas, so that they will be displayed as currency, with two decimal places. To do this,

Place your cursor on C9 and type:

/R   starts RANGE command

F   selects Format option

C   selects Currency option and displays # of decimal places: 2

RETURN   displays Range to format: C9

Move cursor, with arrow keys, to C13. Notice the screen is reversing to show you which coordinates are to be formatted.

RETURN   executes the command

Your worksheet should now look like Figure 1.

MAKING WORKSHEET ENTRIES

_________ NOTE _________

> Never enter values into coordinates containing formulas, or the formulas will be erased.

Now that you have entered all the formulas, make your worksheet entries, above the double-dashed line, as illustrated in Figure 2.

```
           A        B        C

 1 Gross Income %            0.25
 2 Monthly Income            2700
 3 Interest Rate             0.12
 4 No.of Comp.Periods          12
 5 Term                        30
 6 Down Payment %            0.15
 7 Tax & Insurance %          0.3
 8                      =============
 9 Min. Loan Payment      $519.23
10 Max. Loan Payment      $675.00
11 Loan Amount         $50,478.75
12 Purchase Price      $59,386.76
13 Down Payment         $8,908.01
```

Figure 2

Now that your worksheet is complete, it is ready and all you need to do is enter your own set of known values.

SAVING YOUR WORKSHEET

Now save your worksheet for future use, so that the next time you wish to figure these computations all you will need to do is enter in your new known values, and you will not need to retype in the labels or enter the formulas.

To save your worksheet, place a formatted data diskette in Drive A.

With your cursor on any location, type:

/F	starts FILE command
S	selects Save option

Type in name of file.

RETURN	executes the command

PRINTING YOUR WORKSHEET

To print all or a portion of your worksheet, use the following directions, which are given for the Epson printer (compressed font).

Place your cursor on A1 and type:

/P	starts PRINT command
P	displays options
O	selects Options option
S	Selects Setup option and displays: Enter Setup String
\015	sets an Epson printer to compressed font
RETURN	accepts setup and displays options
M	selects Margin option
R	selects Right option
230	characters per line
RETURN	displays options
Q	selects Quit option and returns to main print menu
R	displays Range to print from
.	ellipsis - indicates from-to

Move cursor, with arrow keys, to last coordinate in area you wish to print. The screen will reverse to indicate the area being printed.

RETURN	executes the command
G	selects Go option and prints

To exit out of PRINT command, type:

Q	selects Quit option and exits out of PRINT command

LOADING YOUR WORKSHEET BACK INTO LOTUS 1-2-3

At a later date, when you need to use the worksheet to do further computations, just load your worksheet back into memory.

To do this, you must first clear memory if there is anything in it. To clear the memory,

Leave your cursor on any location and type:

/W   starts WORKSHEET command

E   selects Erase option

Y   Yes, to confirm

Now you are ready to load the worksheet into the memory, using 1-2-3's FILE command. To do this,

Place the data diskette from which you wish to load into Drive A.

Leave your cursor on any location and type:

/F   starts FILE command

R   selects Retrieve option

Place your cursor on the file name you wish to load, and press:

RETURN   executes the command

CHAPTER TWO

SIMPLE INTEREST ON A SAVINGS ACCOUNT

DESCRIPTION

When money is deposited in a savings account, the lending institution pays you for the use of your money. When computing simple interest, five factors must be taken into consideration:

1. The amount of the principal.

2. The interest rate percentage.

3. The length of time the money is left in your bank account.

4. The type of interest, i.e., the manner in which the lending institution computes the interest. If the interest they pay is computed on the original amount of the principal only, it is called simple interest.

5. The number of periods per year when interest will be calculated.

EXAMPLE

If you deposit $358,000 in a savings account for a period of three years, in a bank which pays 6.3% annual simple interest, how much would your savings account be worth at the end of the 3 year period?

SETTING UP YOUR WORKSHEET - ENTERING LABELS

USE THE FOLLOWING STEP-BY-STEP DIRECTIONS FOR ENTERING THE LABELS IN
FIGURE 1:

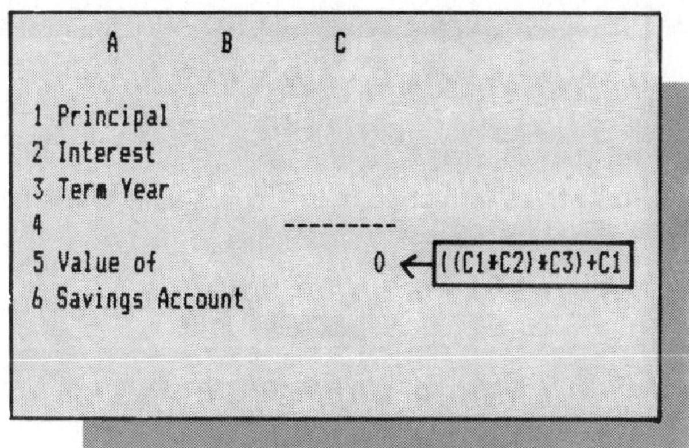

Figure 1

Enter your labels, starting in A1, and continuing through A6, exactly as illustrated in Figure 1, retaining exact row and column locations of all information.

Next enter the dashed line in row 4.

Place your cursor on C4 and type:

  \\   starts REPEAT command

  —   label to be repeated

  `RETURN`   executes the command

Now that you have entered your labels and the dashed line, you will enter the formula which will
calculate the unknown value.

ENTERING THE FORMULA

USE THE FOLLOWING STEP-BY-STEP DIRECTIONS FOR ENTERING THE FORMULA
WHICH WILL CALCULATE THE UNKNOWN VALUE:

The formula in column C, underneath the dashed line, will compute the value of the savings account after 3 years.

Place your cursor on C5 and type:

((C 1 * C 2) * C 3) + C 1   formula

RETURN   enters the formula

Your worksheet should look like Figure 1.

MAKING WORKSHEET ENTRIES

NOTE

Never enter values into coordinates containing formulas, or the formulas will be erased.

Now that you have entered the formula, make your worksheet entries, above the dashed line, as illustrated in Figure 2.

```
            A        B        C

1 Principal                 358000
2 Interest                   0.063
3 Term Year                      3
4                        ---------
5 Value of                  425662
6 Savings Account

                 Figure 2
```

Figure 2

Now that your worksheet is complete, it is ready and all you need to do is enter your own set of known values.

SAVING YOUR WORKSHEET

Now save your worksheet for future use, so that the next time you wish to figure these computations all you will need to do is enter in your new known values, and you will not need to retype in the labels or enter the formulas.

To save your worksheet, place a formatted data diskette in Drive A.

With your cursor on any location, type:

/F	starts FILE command
S	selects Save option

Type in name of file.

RETURN	executes the command

PRINTING YOUR WORKSHEET

To print all or a portion of your worksheet, use the following directions, which are given for the Epson printer (compressed font).

Place your cursor on A1 and type:

/P	starts PRINT command
P	displays options
O	selects Options option
S	Selects Setup option and displays: Enter Setup String
\015	sets an Epson printer to compressed font
RETURN	accepts setup and displays options
M	selects Margin option
R	selects Right option
230	characters per line
RETURN	displays options
Q	selects Quit option and returns to main print menu
R	displays Range to print from
.	ellipsis - indicates from-to

Move cursor, with arrow keys, to last coordinate in area you wish to print. The screen will reverse to indicate the area being printed.

RETURN	executes the command
G	selects Go option and prints

To exit out of PRINT command, type:

Q	selects Quit option and exits out of PRINT command

LOADING YOUR WORKSHEET BACK INTO LOTUS 1-2-3

At a later date, when you need to use the worksheet to do further computations, just load your worksheet back into memory.

To do this, you must first clear memory if there is anything in it. To clear the memory,

Leave your cursor on any location and type:

/W	starts WORKSHEET command
E	selects Erase option
Y	Yes, to confirm

Now you are ready to load the worksheet into the memory, using 1-2-3's FILE command. To do this,

Place the data diskette from which you wish to load into Drive A.

Leave your cursor on any location and type:

/F	starts FILE command
R	selects Retrieve option

Place your cursor on the file name you wish to load, and press:

RETURN	executes the command

CHAPTER THREE

COMPOUND INTEREST ON A SAVINGS ACCOUNT

DESCRIPTION

When you deposit money in a savings account, the lending institution usually pays you compound interest. This means that you will not only earn interest on the original amount of the principal, but also on the interest that has been earned in each previous compounding period and left in the account.

When computing the compound interest four factors must be taken into consideration:

1. The amount of the principal.

2. The interest rate percentage.

3. The length of time the money is left in your bank account.

4. The number of compounding periods per year.

EXAMPLE

If you deposit $358,000 in a savings account in a bank which will compound the interest at an annual interest rate of 6% compounded annually for a period of 3 years, what will your account be worth at the end of the 3-year period?

SETTING UP YOUR WORKSHEET - ENTERING LABELS

USE THE FOLLOWING STEP-BY-STEP DIRECTIONS FOR ENTERING THE LABELS IN
FIGURE 1:

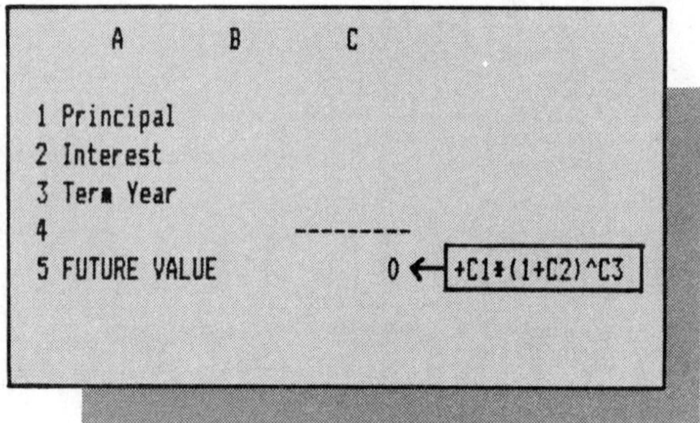

Figure 1

Enter your labels, starting in A1 and continuing through A5, exactly as illustrated in Figure 1, retaining exact row and column locations of all information.

Next enter the dashed line in row 4.

Place your cursor on C4 and type:

\	starts REPEAT command
—	label to be repeated
RETURN	executes the command

Now that you have entered your labels and the dashed line, you will enter the formula which will
calculate the unknown value.

ENTERING THE FORMULA

USE THE FOLLOWING STEP-BY-STEP DIRECTIONS FOR ENTERING THE FORMULA
WHICH WILL CALCULATE THE UNKNOWN VALUE:

The formula in column C, beneath the dashed line, to the right of FUTURE VALUE, will compute
the future value of a savings account.

Place your cursor on C5 and type:

+ C 1 * (1 + C 2)^C 3   formula

RETURN   enters the formula

Your worksheet should now look like Figure 1.

MAKING WORKSHEET ENTRIES

___ **NOTE** ___

Never enter values into coordinates containing formulas, or the
formulas will be erased.

Now that you have entered the formula, make your worksheet entries, above the dashed line, as illustrated in Figure 2.

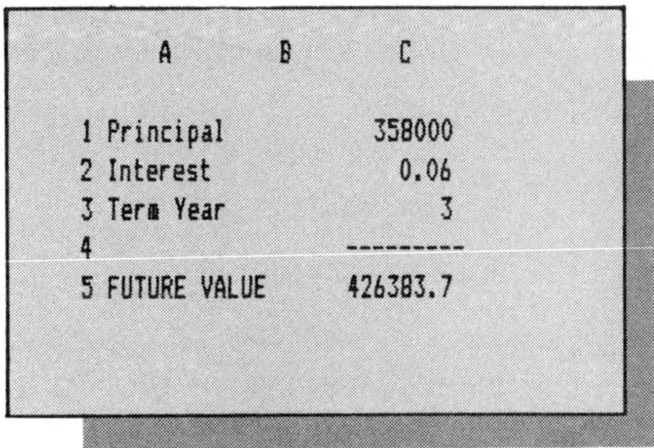

Figure 2

Now that your worksheet is complete, it is ready and all you need to do is enter your own set of known values.

SAVING YOUR WORKSHEET

Now save your worksheet for future use, so that the next time you wish to figure these computation all you will need to do is enter in your new known values, and you will not need to retype in the labels or enter the formula.

To save your worksheet, place a formatted data diskette in Drive A.

With your cursor on any location, type:

/F	starts FILE command
S	selects Save option

Type in name of file.

RETURN	executes the command

PRINTING YOUR WORKSHEET

To print all or a portion of your worksheet, use the following directions, which are given for the Epson printer (compressed font).

Place your cursor on A1 and type:

/P	starts PRINT command
P	displays options
O	selects Options option
S	Selects Setup option and displays: Enter Setup String
\015	sets an Epson printer to compressed font
RETURN	accepts setup and displays options
M	selects Margin option
R	selects Right option
230	characters per line
RETURN	displays options

Q	selects Quit option and returns to main print menu
R	displays Range to print from
.	ellipsis - indicates from-to

Move cursor, with arrow keys, to last coordinate in area you wish to print. The screen will reverse to indicate the area being printed.

| RETURN | executes the command |
| G | selects Go option and prints |

To exit out of PRINT command, type:

| Q | selects Quit option and exits out of PRINT command |

LOADING YOUR WORKSHEET BACK INTO LOTUS 1-2-3

At a later date, when you need to use the worksheet to do further computations, just load your worksheet back into memory.

To do this, you must first clear memory if there is anything in it. To clear the memory,

Leave your cursor on any location and type:

/W	starts WORKSHEET command
E	selects Erase option
Y	Yes, to confirm

Now you are ready to load the worksheet into the memory, using 1-2-3's FILE command. To do this,

Place the data diskette from which you wish to load into Drive A.

Leave your cursor on any location and type:

| /F | starts FILE command |
| R | selects Retrieve option |

Place your cursor on the file name you wish to load, and press:

| RETURN | executes the command |

CHAPTER FOUR

PRESENT VALUE WITH CONTINUOUS COMPOUNDING

DESCRIPTION

Continuous compounding means that the interest is computed continuously during the period. To determine the present value of a business, the revenue generated each year must be considered, along with the discount rate and the method of computing it.

EXAMPLE

Aroma Coffee Corporation has coffee vending machines disbursed widely throughout the city. Each machine generates $6,000 in revenue every year. The discount rate is 12% annual with continuous compounding.

What would the present value be of four years' operation of each machine (before taxes, insurance, maintenance expenses, etc.)?

SETTING UP YOUR WORKSHEET - ENTERING LABELS

USE THE FOLLOWING STEP-BY-STEP DIRECTIONS FOR ENTERING THE LABELS IN
FIGURE 1:

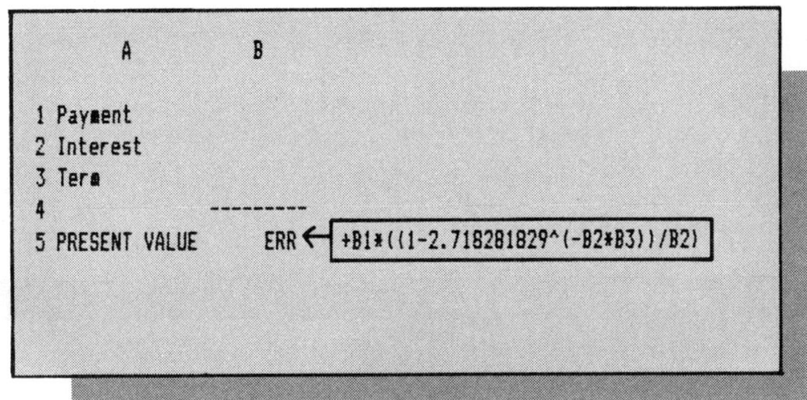

Figure 1

First you will expand column A to 14 characters. To do this,

Place your cursor on column A and type:

/W	starts WORKSHEET command
C	selects Column-Width option
S	selects Set option
14	number of spaces in column
RETURN	executes the command

Now enter your labels, starting in A1 and continuing through A5, exactly as illustrated in Figure 1,
retaining exact row and column locations of all information.

Next enter the dashed line in row 4.

Place your cursor on B4 and type:

\	starts REPEAT command
—	label to be repeated
RETURN	executes the command

Now that you have entered your labels and the dashed line, you will enter the formula which will
calculate the unknown value.

ENTERING THE FORMULA

USE THE FOLLOWING STEP-BY-STEP DIRECTIONS FOR ENTERING THE FORMULA WHICH WILL CALCULATE THE UNKNOWN VALUE:

The formula you are about to enter will calculate the present value.

Place your cursor on B5 and type:

+ B 1 * ((1 — 2.718281829 ^ (— B 2 * B 3)) / B 2)   formula

RETURN   enters the formula

Your worksheet should now look like Figure 1.

MAKING WORKSHEET ENTRIES

_______________________ **NOTE** _______________________

Never enter values into coordinates containing formulas, or the formulas will be erased.

Now that you have entered all the formulas, make your worksheet entries, above the dashed line, into rows 1, 2 and 3, as illustrated in Figure 2.

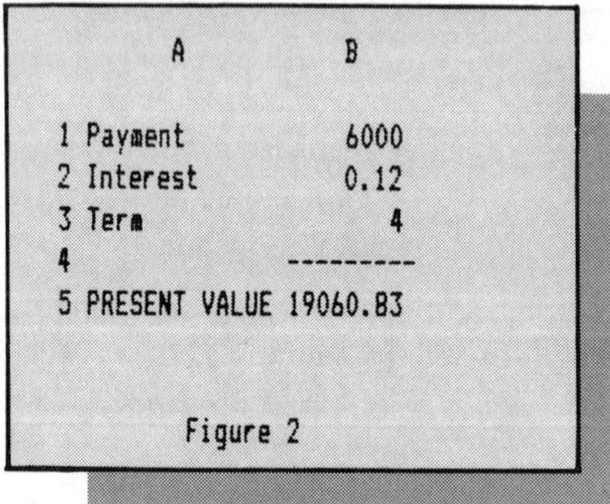

Figure 2

Now that your worksheet is complete, it is ready and all you need to do is enter your own set of known values.

SAVING YOUR WORKSHEET

Now save your worksheet for future use, so that the next time you wish to figure these computations all you will need to do is enter in your new known values, and you will not need to retype in the labels or enter the formulas.

To save your worksheet, place a formatted data diskette in Drive A.

With your cursor on any location, type:

/F	starts FILE command
S	selects Save option

Type in name of file.

RETURN	executes the command

PRINTING YOUR WORKSHEET

To print all or a portion of your worksheet, use the following directions, which are given for the Epson printer (compressed font).

Place your cursor on A1 and type:

/P	starts PRINT command
P	displays options
O	selects Options option
S	Selects Setup option and displays: Enter Setup String
\015	sets an Epson printer to compressed font
RETURN	accepts setup and displays options
M	selects Margin option
R	selects Right option
230	characters per line
RETURN	displays options

Q	selects Quit option and returns to main print menu
R	displays Range to print from
.	ellipsis - indicates from-to

Move cursor, with arrow keys, to last coordinate in area you wish to print. The screen will reverse to indicate the area being printed.

RETURN	executes the command
G	selects Go option and prints

To exit out of PRINT command, type:

Q	selects Quit option and exits out of PRINT command

LOADING YOUR WORKSHEET BACK INTO LOTUS 1-2-3

At a later date, when you need to use the worksheet to do further computations, just load your worksheet back into memory.

To do this, you must first clear memory if there is anything in it. To clear the memory,

Leave your cursor on any location and type:

/W	starts WORKSHEET command
E	selects Erase option
Y	Yes, to confirm

Now you are ready to load the worksheet into the memory, using 1-2-3's FILE command. To do this,

Place the data diskette from which you wish to load into Drive A.

Leave your cursor on any location and type:

/F	starts FILE command
R	selects Retrieve option

Place your cursor on the file name you wish to load, and press:

RETURN	executes the command

CHAPTER FIVE

FUTURE VALUE WITH CONTINUOUS COMPOUNDING

DESCRIPTION

Continuous compounding means that the interest is computed continuously during the period. To determine the future value of a series of yearly payments which are deposited in an account for five years, it is necessary to determine the amount of the yearly payments, the rate of interest, and the method of computing interest.

EXAMPLE

For a five year period, Mr. Abernathy will be able to deposit $1,500 each year into an account. The payments will be compounded continuously at a rate of 6.5% annually.

What will the value of the payments be at the end of five years?

SETTING UP YOUR WORKSHEET - ENTERING LABELS

USE THE FOLLOWING STEP-BY-STEP DIRECTIONS FOR ENTERING THE LABELS IN FIGURE 1:

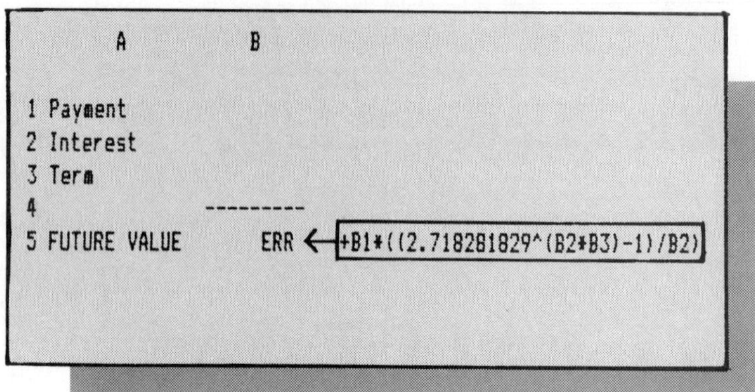

Figure 1

First you will expand column A to 14 characters. To do this,

Place your cursor on column A and type:

/W	starts WORKSHEET command
C	selects Column-Width option
S	selects Set option
14	number of spaces in column
RETURN	executes the command

Now enter your labels, starting in A1 and continuing through A5, exactly as illustrated in Figure 1, retaining exact row and column locations of all information.

Next enter the dashed line in row 4.

Place your cursor on B4 and type:

\	starts REPEAT command
—	label to be repeated
RETURN	executes the command

Now that you have entered your labels and the dashed line, you will begin entering the formula which will calculate the unknown value.

ENTERING THE FORMULA

USE THE FOLLOWING STEP-BY-STEP DIRECTIONS FOR ENTERING THE FORMULA WHICH WILL CALCULATE THE UNKNOWN VALUE:

The formula, in column B, to the right of FUTURE VALUE, will calculate the future value for an annuity invested in even amounts over a 5 year period, with continuous compounding of interest.

Place your cursor on B5 and type:

+ B 1 * ((2.718281829 ^(B 2 * B 3) — 1) / B 2)   formula

| RETURN | enters the formula

Now you will format the coordinate into which you have entered the formula so that it will be displayed with two decimal places.

Leave your cursor on B5 and type:

/R   starts RANGE command

F   selects Format option

F   selects Fixed option and displays number of decimal places: 2

| RETURN | displays Range to format: B5

| RETURN | executes the command

Your worksheet should now look like Figure 1.

MAKING WORKSHEET ENTRIES

```
____________________ NOTE ____________________

Never enter values into coordinates containing formulas, or the
formulas will be erased.
```

Now that you have entered all the formulas, make your worksheet entries, above the double-dashed line into rows 1, 2 and 3, , as illustrated in Figure 2.

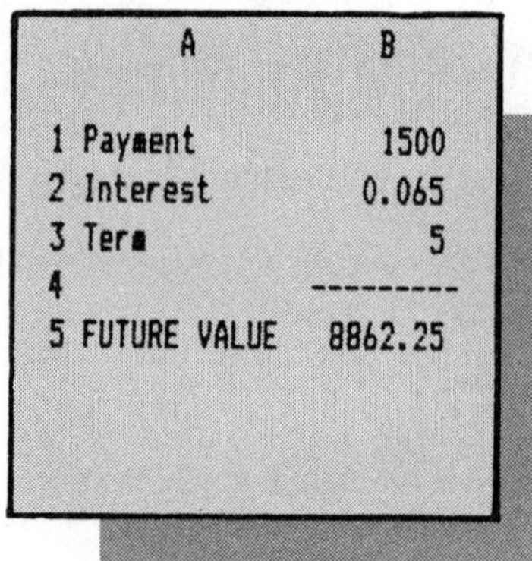

Figure 2

Now that your worksheet is complete, it is ready and all you need to do is enter your own set of known values.

SAVING YOUR WORKSHEET

Now save your worksheet for future use, so that the next time you wish to figure these computations all you will need to do is enter in your new known values, and you will not need to retype in the labels or enter the formulas.

To save your worksheet, place a formatted data diskette in Drive A.

With your cursor on any location, type:

/F   starts FILE command

S   selects Save option

Type in name of file.

RETURN   executes the command

PRINTING YOUR WORKSHEET

To print all or a portion of your worksheet, use the following directions, which are given for the Epson printer (compressed font).

Place your cursor on A1 and type:

/P	starts PRINT command
P	displays options
O	selects Options option
S	Selects Setup option and displays: Enter Setup String
\015	sets an Epson printer to compressed font
RETURN	accepts setup and displays options
M	selects Margin option
R	selects Right option
230	characters per line
RETURN	displays options
Q	selects Quit option and returns to main print menu
R	displays Range to print from
.	ellipsis - indicates from-to

Move cursor, with arrow keys, to last coordinate in area you wish to print. The screen will reverse to indicate the area being printed.

RETURN	executes the command
G	selects Go option and prints

To exit out of PRINT command, type:

Q	selects Quit option and exits out of PRINT command

LOADING YOUR WORKSHEET BACK INTO LOTUS 1-2-3

At a later date, when you need to use the worksheet to do further computations, just load your worksheet back into memory.

To do this, you must first clear memory if there is anything in it. To clear the memory,

Leave your cursor on any location and type:

/W   starts WORKSHEET command

E   selects Erase option

Y   Yes, to confirm

Now you are ready to load the worksheet into the memory, using 1-2-3's FILE command. To do this,

Place the data diskette from which you wish to load into Drive A.

Leave your cursor on any location and type:

/F   starts FILE command

R   selects Retrieve option

Place your cursor on the file name you wish to load, and press:

RETURN   executes the command

CHAPTER SIX

FINDING PV FROM FV CONTINUOUS COMPOUNDING

DESCRIPTION

Continuous compounding means that the compounding takes place continuously over the time periods, rather than at the end of each period. In this exercise, you will determine the unknown present value from the known future value. You will use Euler's constant, which is a constant used in computing continuous compounding.

EXAMPLE

Mr. Huber wants to accumulate $10,500 in his savings account at the end of 6 years. The annual rate of interest is 8.5% compounded continuously.

What is the present value of his savings account, i.e., how much money should he deposit now in order to accumulate the $10,500 at the end of 6 years.

SETTING UP YOUR WORKSHEET - ENTERING LABELS

USE THE FOLLOWING STEP-BY-STEP DIRECTIONS FOR ENTERING THE LABELS IN FIGURE 1:

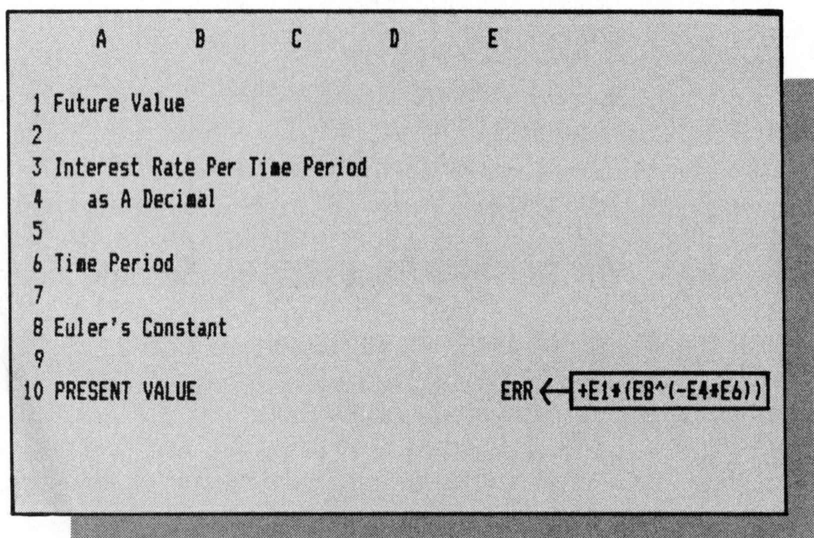

Figure 1

Enter your labels, starting in A1 and continuing through A10, exactly as illustrated in Figure 1, retaining exact row and column locations of all information.

Now that you have entered your labels, you will enter the formulas which will calculate the unknown value.

ENTERING THE FORMULA

USE THE FOLLOWING STEP-BY-STEP DIRECTIONS FOR ENTERING THE FORMULA WHICH WILL CALCULATE THE UNKNOWN VALUE.

Formula one, in column E, to the right of PRESENT VALUE, will calculate the Present Value.

Place your cursor on E10 and type:

+ E 1 * (E 8 ^ (— E 4 * E 6))   formula

RETURN   enters the formula

Now you will format the coordinate into which you have entered the formula so that it will be displayed with two decimal places.

Leave your cursor on E10 and type:

/R	starts RANGE command
F	selects Format option
F	selects Fixed option and displays number of decimal places: 2
RETURN	displays Range to format: E10
RETURN	executes the command

Your worksheet should now look like Figure 1.

MAKING WORKSHEET ENTRIES

_______________ **NOTE** _______________

Never enter values into coordinates containing formulas, or the formulas will be erased.

Now that you have entered all the formulas, make your worksheet entries, in Column E, in Rows 1, 4, 6 and 8, as illustrated in Figure 2.

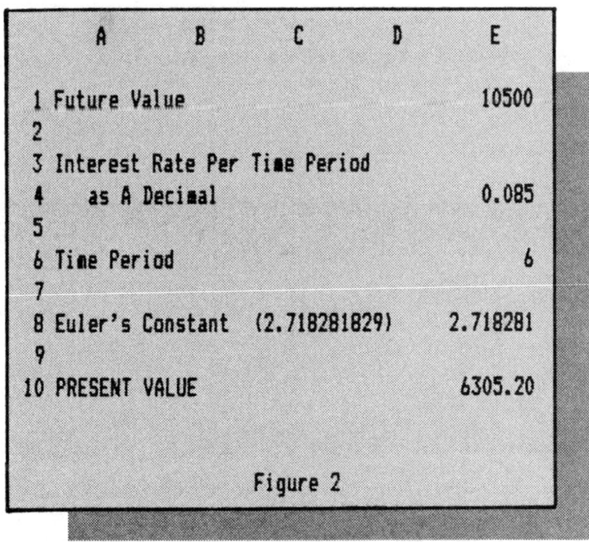

Figure 2

Now that your worksheet is complete, it is ready and all you need to do is enter your own set of known values.

SAVING YOUR WORKSHEET

Now save your worksheet for future use, so that the next time you wish to figure these computations all you will need to do is enter in your new known values, and you will not need to retype in the labels or enter the formulas.

To save your worksheet, place a formatted data diskette in Drive A.

With your cursor on any location, type:

/F	starts FILE command
S	selects Save option

Type in name of file.

RETURN	executes the command

PRINTING YOUR WORKSHEET

To print all or a portion of your worksheet, use the following directions, which are given for the Epson printer (compressed font).

Place your cursor on A1 and type:

/P	starts PRINT command
P	displays options
O	selects Options option
S	Selects Setup option and displays: Enter Setup String
\015	sets an Epson printer to compressed font
RETURN	accepts setup and displays options
M	selects Margin option
R	selects Right option
230	characters per line
RETURN	displays options
Q	selects Quit option and returns to main print menu
R	displays Range to print from
.	ellipsis - indicates from-to

Move cursor, with arrow keys, to last coordinate in area you wish to print. The screen will reverse to indicate the area being printed.

RETURN	executes the command
G	selects Go option and prints

To exit out of PRINT command, type:

Q	selects Quit option and exits out of PRINT command

LOADING YOUR WORKSHEET BACK INTO LOTUS 1-2-3

At a later date, when you need to use the worksheet to do further computations, just load your worksheet back into memory.

To do this, you must first clear memory if there is anything in it. To clear the memory,

Leave your cursor on any location and type:

/W	starts WORKSHEET command
E	selects Erase option
Y	Yes, to confirm

Now you are ready to load the worksheet into the memory, using 1-2-3's FILE command. To do this,

Place the data diskette from which you wish to load into Drive A.

Leave your cursor on any location and type:

/F	starts FILE command
R	selects Retrieve option

Place your cursor on the file name you wish to load, and press:

RETURN	executes the command

CHAPTER SEVEN

FINDING FV FROM PV CONTINUOUS COMPOUNDING

DESCRIPTION

Continuous compounding means that the compounding takes place continuously over the time periods, rather than at the end of each period. In this exercise, you will determine the unknown future value from the known present value. You will use Euler's constant, which is a constant used in computing continuous compounding.

EXAMPLE

If $5,000 is invested in a savings accouant at a bank which pays 6% interest, compounded continuously, what will be the future value of the account at the end of a 3-year period?

SETTING UP YOUR WORKSHEET - ENTERING LABELS

USE THE FOLLOWING STEP-BY-STEP DIRECTIONS FOR ENTERING THE LABELS IN
FIGURE 1:

```
         A        B       C       D       E

 1 Present Value
 2
 3 Time Period
 4
 5 Euler's Constant (2.718281829)
 6
 7 Interest Rate Per Time Period
 8    As A Decimal                            0.005 ←  0.06/12
 9
10 FUTURE VALUE                               ERR ← +E1*(E5^(E8*E3))
```

Figure 1

Enter your labels, starting in A1 and continuing through A10, exactly as illustrated in Figure 1, retaining exact row and column locations of all information.

Now that you have entered your labels, you will enter the formulas which will calculate the unknown values.

ENTERING THE FORMULAS

USE THE FOLLOWING STEP-BY-STEP DIRECTIONS FOR ENTERING THE FORMULAS
WHICH WILL CALCULATE THE UNKNOWN VALUES.

Formula one, in column E, computes the Interest Rate Per Time Period As A Decimal.

Place your cursor on E8 and type:

0.06/12	formula for interest rate
RETURN	enters the formula

Formula two, in column E, computes the Future Value.

Place your cursor on E10 and type:

+ E 1 * (E 5 ^ (E 8 * E 3))	formula
RETURN	enters the formula

Now you will format the coordinate into which you have entered the formula so that it will be
displayed with two decimal places.

Leave your cursor on E10 and type:

/R	starts RANGE command
F	selects Format option
F	selects Fixed option and displays number of decimal places: 2
RETURN	displays Range to format: E10
RETURN	executes the command

Your worksheet should now look like Figure 1.

MAKING WORKSHEET ENTRIES

___ **NOTE** ___

Never enter values into cells containing formulas, or the formulas will be erased.

Now that you have entered all the formulas, make your worksheet entries, in Column E, in Rows 1, 3 and 5, as illustrated in Figure 2.

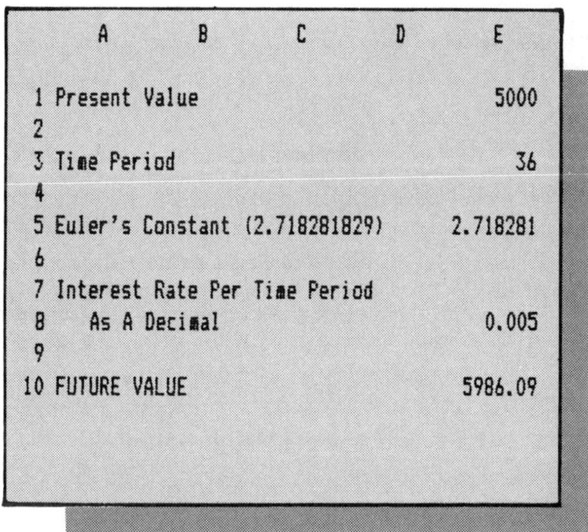

Figure 2

Now that your worksheet is complete, it is ready and all you need to do is enter your own set of known values.

SAVING YOUR WORKSHEET

Now save your worksheet for future use, so that the next time you wish to figure these computation all you will need to do is enter in your new known values, and you will not need to retype in the labels or enter the formula.

To save your worksheet, place a formatted data diskette in Drive A.

With your cursor on any location, type:

/F	starts FILE command
S	selects Save option

Type in name of file.

RETURN	executes the command

PRINTING YOUR WORKSHEET

To print all or a portion of your worksheet, use the following directions, which are given for the Epson printer (compressed font).

Place your cursor on A1 and type:

/P	starts PRINT command
P	displays options
O	selects Options option
S	Selects Setup option and displays: Enter Setup String
\015	sets an Epson printer to compressed font
RETURN	accepts setup and displays options
M	selects Margin option
R	selects Right option
230	characters per line
RETURN	displays options
Q	selects Quit option and returns to main print menu
R	displays Range to print from
.	ellipsis - indicates from-to

Move cursor, with arrow keys, to last coordinate in area you wish to print. The screen will reverse to indicate the area being printed.

RETURN	executes the command
G	selects Go option and prints

To exit out of PRINT command, type:

Q	selects Quit option and exits out of PRINT command

LOADING YOUR WORKSHEET BACK INTO LOTUS 1-2-3

At a later date, when you need to use the worksheet to do further computations, just load your worksheet back into memory.

To do this, you must first clear memory if there is anything in it. To clear the memory,

Leave your cursor on any location and type:

/W   starts WORKSHEET command

E   selects Erase option

Y   Yes, to confirm

Now you are ready to load the worksheet into the memory, using 1-2-3's FILE command. To do this,

Place the data diskette from which you wish to load into Drive A.

Leave your cursor on any location and type:

/F   starts FILE command

R   selects Retrieve option

Place your cursor on the file name you wish to load, and press:

RETURN   executes the command

CHAPTER EIGHT

GENERAL ANNUITY DUE (SOLVING FOR CASH PAYMENT PRESENT VALUE)

DESCRIPTION

An annuity due involves payments made at the beginning of each payment period. Most leases are considered an annuity due.

EXAMPLE

You own farmland which has a present value of $100,000, and want to lease it to a soy bean grower for 25 years. You want to earn an annual return of 18% annual interest, compounded quarterly. The soy bean grower will make his lease payments annually at the beginning of each year.

What will be the amount of the annual payments to you?

SETTING UP YOUR WORKSHEET - ENTERING LABELS

USE THE FOLLOWING STEP-BY-STEP DIRECTIONS FOR ENTERING THE LABELS IN
FIGURE 1.

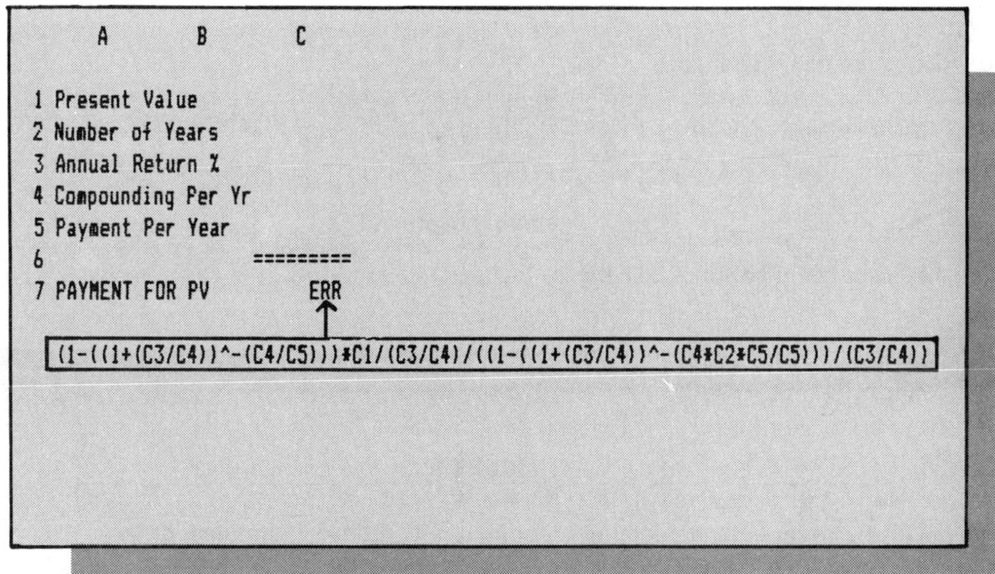

Figure 1

Enter your labels, starting in A1 and continuing through A7, exactly as illustrated in Figure 1, retaining exact row and column locations of all information.

Next enter the double-dashed line in row 6.

Place your cursor on C6 and type:

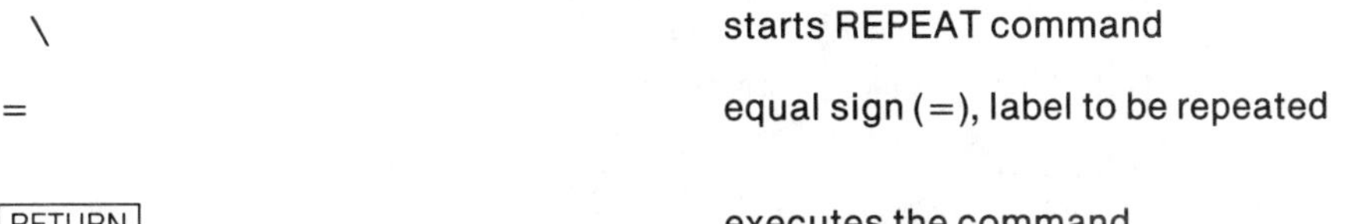

\	starts REPEAT command
=	equal sign (=), label to be repeated
RETURN	executes the command

Now that you have entered your labels and the double-dashed line, you will enter the formula which
will calculate the unknown value.

ENTERING THE FORMULA

USE THE FOLLOWING STEP-BY-STEP DIRECTIONS FOR ENTERING THE FORMULA WHICH WILL CALCULATE THE UNKNOWN VALUE.

The formula, in column C, to the right of PAYMENT FOR PV, calculates the present value payment.

Place your cursor on C7 and type:

(1—((1+(C3/C4))^—(C4/C5)))*C1/(C3/C4)/((1—((1+(C3/C4))^—((C4*C2*C5/C5)))/(C3/C4)) formula

RETURN   enters the formula

Your worksheet should now look like Figure 1.

MAKING WORKSHEET ENTRIES

___________________________ NOTE ___________________________

Never enter values into coordinates containing formulas, or the formulas will be erased.

Now that you have entered all the formulas, make your worksheet entries, above the double-dashed line, in rows 1, 2, 3, 4 and 5, as illustrated in Figure 2.

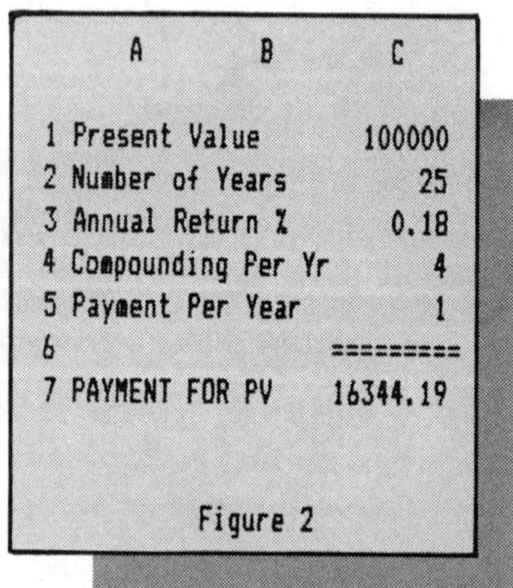

Figure 2

Now that your worksheet is complete, it is ready and all you need to do is enter your own set of known values.

SAVING YOUR WORKSHEET

Now save your worksheet for future use, so that the next time you wish to figure these computations all you will need to do is enter in your new known values, and you will not need to retype in the labels or enter the formulas.

To save your worksheet, place a formatted data diskette in Drive A.

With your cursor on any location, type:

/F	starts FILE command
S	selects Save option

Type in name of file.

RETURN	executes the command

PRINTING YOUR WORKSHEET

To print all or a portion of your worksheet, use the following directions, which are given for the Epson printer (compressed font).

Place your cursor on A1 and type:

/P	starts PRINT command
P	displays options
O	selects Options option
S	Selects Setup option and displays: Enter Setup String
\015	sets an Epson printer to compressed font
RETURN	accepts setup and displays options
M	selects Margin option
R	selects Right option
230	characters per line
RETURN	displays options
Q	selects Quit option and returns to main print menu
R	displays Range to print from
.	ellipsis - indicates from-to

Move cursor, with arrow keys, to last coordinate in area you wish to print. The screen will reverse to indicate the area being printed.

| RETURN | executes the command |

G   selects Go option and prints

To exit out of PRINT command, type:

Q   selects Quit option and exits out of PRINT command

LOADING YOUR WORKSHEET BACK INTO LOTUS 1-2-3

At a later date, when you need to use the worksheet to do further computations, just load your worksheet back into memory.

To do this, you must first clear memory if there is anything in it. To clear the memory,

Leave your cursor on any location and type:

/W   starts WORKSHEET command

E   selects Erase option

Y   Yes, to confirm

Now you are ready to load the worksheet into the memory, using 1-2-3's FILE command. To do this,

Place the data diskette from which you wish to load into Drive A.

Leave your cursor on any location and type:

/F   starts FILE command

R   selects Retrieve option

Place your cursor on the file name you wish to load, and press:

| RETURN | executes the command |

CHAPTER NINE

GENERAL ANNUITY DUE SOLVING FOR WEEKLY CASH PAYMENT

DESCRIPTION

To calculate the weekly cash payment required as a deposit at the beginning of each week, in order to accumulate a specified amount of money in a savings account at the end of a 3-year period, the annual interest percentage the bank pays, and the number of compounding periods in a year must be considered.

EXAMPLE

Your goal is to accumulate $5000 in your savings account at the end of three years. You plan on making weekly deposits every Monday for the three-year period. Your savings account draws 6.5% annual interest and is compounded monthly.

How much should your weekly deposit be in order to reach your goal of accumulating $5000 at the end of three years?

SETTING UP YOUR WORKSHEET - ENTERING LABELS

USE THE FOLLOWING STEP-BY-STEP DIRECTIONS FOR ENTERING THE LABELS IN FIGURE 1.

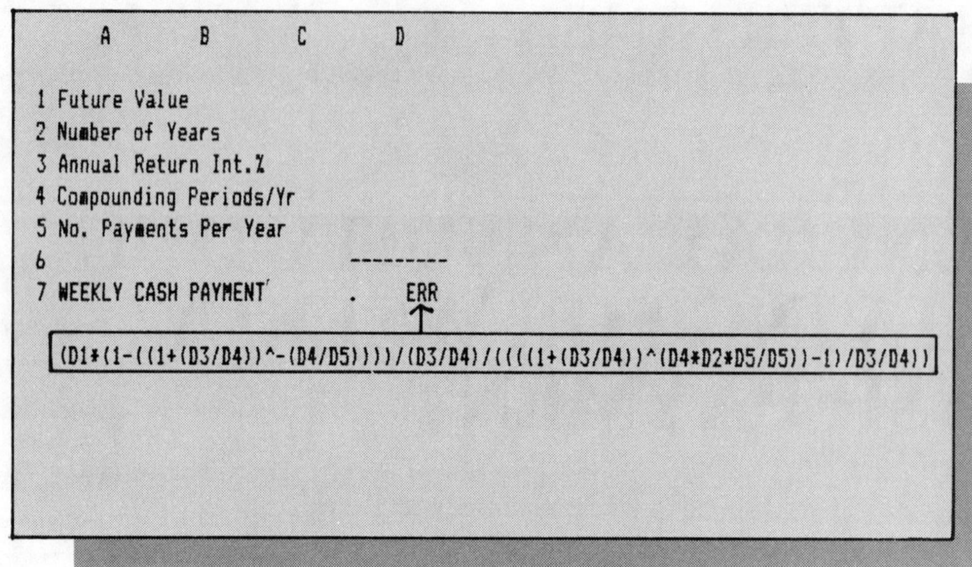

Figure 1

Enter your labels, starting in A1 and continuing through A7, exactly as illustrated in Figure 1, retaining exact row and column locations of all information.

Next enter the dashed line in row 6.

Place your cursor on D6 and type:

\	starts REPEAT command
—	label to be repeated
 RETURN	executes the command

Now that you have entered your labels and the dashed line, you will enter the formula which will calculate the unknown value.

ENTERING THE FORMULA

USE THE FOLLOWING STEP-BY-STEP DIRECTIONS FOR ENTERING THE FORMULA WHICH WILL CALCULATE THE UNKNOWN VALUE.

The formula, in column D, to the right of WEEKLY CASH PAYMENT, below the dashed line, will calculate the weekly cash payment.

Place your cursor on D7 and type:

(D1*(1—((1+(D3/D4))^—(D4/D5))))/(D3/D4)/((((1+(D3/D4))^(D4*D2*D5/D5))—1)/(D3/D4)) formula

| RETURN | enters the formula

Now you will format the coordinate into which you have entered the formula so that it will be displayed with two decimal places.

Leave your cursor on D7 and type:

/R   starts RANGE command

F   selects Format option

F   selects Fixed option and displays number of decimal
                                        places: 2

| RETURN | displays Range to format: D7

| RETURN | executes the command

Your worksheet should now look like Figure 1.

MAKING WORKSHEET ENTRIES

_________________ **NOTE** _________________

> Never enter values into coordinates containing formulas, or the
> formulas will be erased.

Now that you have entered all the formulas, make your worksheet entries, in Column D, above the dashed line, in rows 1, 2, 3, 4 and 5, as illustrated in Figure 2.

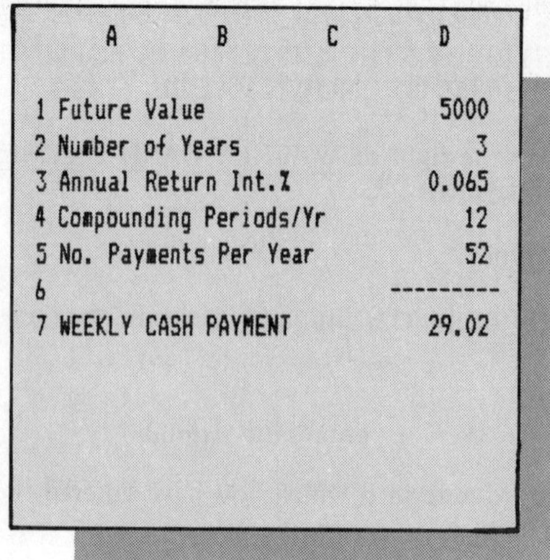

Figure 2

Now that your worksheet is complete, it is ready and all you need to do is enter your own set of known values.

SAVING YOUR WORKSHEET

Now save your worksheet for future use, so that the next time you wish to figure these computations all you will need to do is enter in your new known values, and you will not need to retype in the labels or enter the formulas.

To save your worksheet, place a formatted data diskette in Drive A.

With your cursor on any location, type:

/F   starts FILE command

S   selects Save option

Type in name of file.

RETURN   executes the command

PRINTING YOUR WORKSHEET

To print all or a portion of your worksheet, use the following directions, which are given for the Epson printer (compressed font).

Place your cursor on A1 and type:

/P	starts PRINT command
P	displays options
O	selects Options option
S	Selects Setup option and displays: Enter Setup String
\015	sets an Epson printer to compressed font
RETURN	accepts setup and displays options
M	selects Margin option
R	selects Right option
230	characters per line
RETURN	displays options
Q	selects Quit option and returns to main print menu
R	displays Range to print from
.	ellipsis - indicates from-to

Move cursor, with arrow keys, to last coordinate in area you wish to print. The screen will reverse to indicate the area being printed.

RETURN	executes the command
G	selects Go option and prints

To exit out of PRINT command, type:

Q	selects Quit option and exits out of PRINT command

LOADING YOUR WORKSHEET BACK INTO LOTUS 1-2-3

At a later date, when you need to use the worksheet to do further computations, just load your worksheet back into memory.

To do this, you must first clear memory if there is anything in it. To clear the memory,

Leave your cursor on any location and type:

/W   starts WORKSHEET command

E   selects Erase option

Y   Yes, to confirm

Now you are ready to load the worksheet into the memory, using 1-2-3's FILE command. To do this,

Place the data diskette from which you wish to load into Drive A.

Leave your cursor on any location and type:

/F   starts FILE command

R   selects Retrieve option

Place your cursor on the file name you wish to load, and press:

RETURN   executes the command

CHAPTER TEN

AMORTIZING BOND PREMIUM OR DISCOUNT

In this exercise the bond interest expense is computed by using the effective interest rate times the bond book value, rather than the nominal rate times the par value. The cash paid out, however, is computed using the nominal interest rate times par value.

The difference between the interest expense and cash payment is either the bond premium or the discount. Therefore:

If it is a bond premium, then it is subtracted from the bond book value.

If it is a discount, then it is added to the bond book value.

When computing the interest expense for the next period, the adjusted book value is used.

A company has a bond with a present value of $93204.84. The coupon/year is 2, the number of periods is 20, the nominal interest rate is 7%, the issue is $100,000 and the payment is $3500. The interest yield is 8% and coupon interest is 4%.

They want an amortization schedule set up for 20 periods which will determine the bond interest expense, the bond discount, and the adjusted book value.

SETTING UP YOUR WORKSHEET - ENTERING LABELS

USE THE FOLLOWING STEP-BY-STEP DIRECTIONS FOR ENTERING THE LABELS IN FIGURE 1:

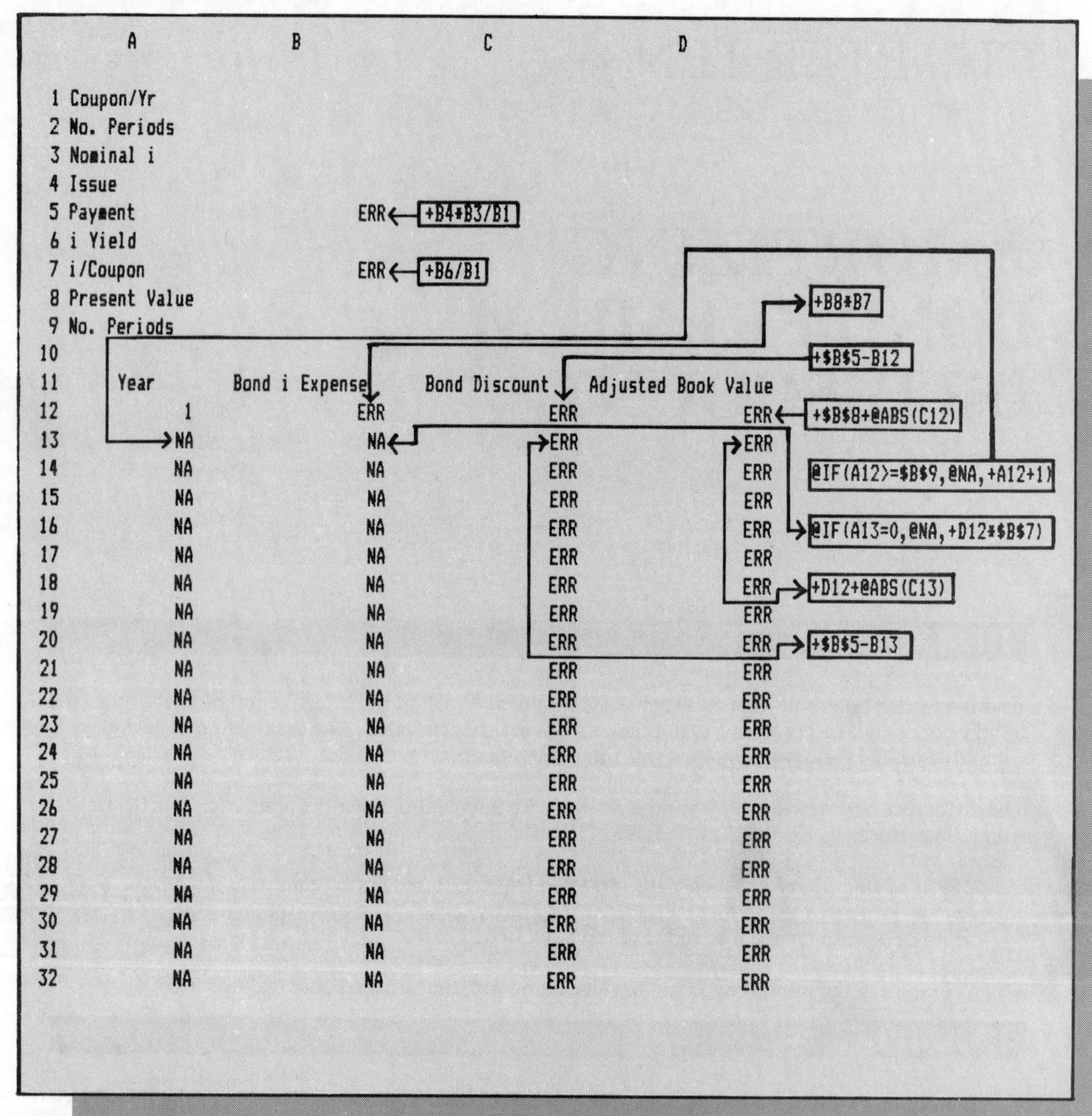

Figure 1

First you will expand all the columns to a width of 20 characters. To do this,

Leave your cursor on any location and type:

/W   starts WORKSHEET command

G   selects Global option

C   selects Column-Width option

20   number of spaces in columns

RETURN   executes the command

Now enter your labels, starting in A1 and continuing through A9, exactly as illustrated in Figure 1, retaining exact row and column locations of all information.

Next enter the labels in row 11. Then you will want to center them. To do this,

Place your cursor on A11 and type:

/R   starts RANGE command

L   selects Label option

C   selects Center option and displays A11

Move your cursor, with the arrow keys, to D11. The screen will reverse to show you the area being centered.

RETURN   executes the command

Now that you have entered your labels, you will begin entering the formulas which will calculate the unknown values.

ENTERING FORMULAS

USE THE FOLLOWING STEP-BY-STEP DIRECTIONS FOR ENTERING THE FORMULAS WHICH WILL CALCULATE THE UNKNOWN VALUES.

Formula one, in column B, to the right of Payment, calculates the payment, by multiplying the issue by the nominal interest, and dividing that by the coupon/yr.

Place your cursor on B5 and type:

+ B 4 * B 3 / B 1   formula

RETURN   enters the formula

Formula two, in column B, to the right of i/Coupon, calculates the interest/coupon by dividing the interest yield by the coupon/yr.

Place your cursor on B7 and type:

+ B 6 / B 1   formula

RETURN   enters the formula

BEFORE ENTERING THE NEXT FORMULA, formula three, enter the value representing the first year. To do this,

Place your cursor on A12 and type:

1   first year

RETURN   enters the value

Now you will enter formula three.

Formula three, in column A, Year, immediately under the 1, which you have just entered, determines that, if the preceding number is greater than or equal to the number of periods (20), it will display an NA. If not, it will add 1 to the preceding number.

NOTE

> 1-2-3 is designed to do one of two things with coordinates when they are copied. The coordinates are either relative to their new location or they remain absolute, which means they remain the same.
>
> A coordinate address is relative unless it is converted to an absolute by having a dollar sign ($) preceding the column designation and/or row designation, i.e. (B9).
>
> A quick way to make a coordinate absolute is by placing your cursor on that coordinate and pressing the F4 key, which will automatically place the dollar as shown.
>
> In formula three, which you are about to enter, the value in B9 must remain absolute, when you copy the formula down the column later. You will note that, in order to accomplish this, when you enter the formula you will be typing B9.

To enter formula three,

Place your cursor on A13 and type:

@ I F (A 1 2 > = $ B $ 9 , @ N A , + A 1 2 + 1)   formula

RETURN   enters the formula

Formula four, in column B, immediately under Bond i Expense, multiplies the present value by the interest/coupon.

Place your cursor on B12 and type:

+ B 8 * B 7   formula

RETURN   enters the formula

Formula five in column C, immediately under Bond Discount, subtracts the bond interest expense from the Payment.

Place your cursor on C12 and type:

+ $ B $ 5 — B 1 2   formula

RETURN   enters the formula

Formula six in column D, immediately under Adjusted Book Value, adds the present value to the bond discount.

Place your cursor on D12 and type:

+ $ B $ 8 + @ A B S (C 1 2)   formula

RETURN   enters the formula

The next set of formulas you are about to enter will all be in ROW 13.

Formula seven in column B, the Bond i Expense column, multiplies the adjusted book value by the interest/coupon.

Place your cursor on B13 and type:

@ I F (A13 = 0 , @ N A , + D12 * $ B $ 7)   formula

RETURN   enters the formula

Formula eight, in column C, the Bond Discount column, subtracts the bond interest expense from the payment.

Place your cursor on C13 and type:

+ $ B $ 5 — B 1 3   formula

RETURN   enters the formula

Formula nine, in column D, Adjusted Book Value column, adds the adjusted book value to the bond discount.

Place your cursor on D13 and type:

+ D 1 2 + @ABS (C 1 3)   formula

RETURN   enters the formula

Now you will format some of the coordinates into which you have entered formulas, so that they will be displayed with two decimal places.

Place your cursor on B12 and type:

/R   starts RANGE command

F   selects Format option

F   selects Fixed option and displays number of decimal places: 2

RETURN   displays Range to format: B12

Move your cursor, with the arrow keys, to D13. The screen will reverse to show you the area being formatted.

RETURN   executes the command

Now that all your formulas have been entered you will copy ONLY THE FORMULAS ENTERED INTO ROW 13, down their respective columns. To do this,

Place your cursor on A13 and type:

/C   starts COPY command and displays Range to copy from: A13, first coordinate to copy from

Move your cursor, with the arrow keys, to D13, which is the last coordinate to copy from. The screen will reverse to show you which coordinates are being copied.

RETURN   displays Range to copy to

A14   first coordinate to copy to

.   ellipsis - indicates from-to

A32   last coordinate to copy to

RETURN   executes the command

Your worksheet should now look like Figure 1.

MAKING WORKSHEET ENTRIES

_______________ **NOTE** _______________

Never enter values into coordinates containing formulas, or the
formulas will be erased.

Now that you have entered all the formulas, make your worksheet entries, into Column B, into
rows 1, 2, 3, 4, 6, 8 and 9 at the top of your worksheet, as illustrated in Figure 2.
Your worksheet should now look like Figure 2.

Now that your worksheet is complete, it is ready and all you need to do is enter your own set of
known values.

SAVING YOUR WORKSHEET

Now save your worksheet for future use, so that the next time you wish to figure these computation
all you will need to do is enter in your new known values, and you will not need to retype in the
labels or enter the formula.

To save your worksheet, place a formatted data diskette in Drive A.

With your cursor on any location, type:

/F   starts FILE command

S   selects Save option

Type in name of file.

RETURN   executes the command

	A	B	C	D
1	Coupon/Yr	2		
2	No. Periods	20		
3	Nominal i	0.07		
4	Issue	100000		
5	Payment	3500		
6	i Yield	0.08		
7	i/Coupon	0.04		
8	Present Value	93204.84		
9	No. Periods	20		
10				
11	Year	Bond i Expense	Bond Discount	Adjusted Book Value
12	1	3728.19	-228.19	93433.03
13	2	3737.32	-237.32	93670.35
14	3	3746.81	-246.81	93917.17
15	4	3756.69	-256.69	94173.86
16	5	3766.95	-266.95	94440.81
17	6	3777.63	-277.63	94718.44
18	7	3788.74	-288.74	95007.18
19	8	3800.29	-300.29	95307.47
20	9	3812.30	-312.30	95619.77
21	10	3824.79	-324.79	95944.56
22	11	3837.78	-337.78	96282.34
23	12	3851.29	-351.29	96633.63
24	13	3865.35	-365.35	96998.98
25	14	3879.96	-379.96	97378.94
26	15	3895.16	-395.16	97774.09
27	16	3910.96	-410.96	98185.06
28	17	3927.40	-427.40	98612.46
29	18	3944.50	-444.50	99056.96
30	19	3962.28	-462.28	99519.24
31	20	3980.77	-480.77	100000.01
32	NA	NA	NA	NA

Figure 2

PRINTING YOUR WORKSHEET

To print all or a portion of your worksheet, use the following directions, which are given for the Epson printer (compressed font).

Place your cursor on A1 and type:

/P	starts PRINT command
P	displays options
O	selects Options option
S	Selects Setup option and displays: Enter Setup String
\015	sets an Epson printer to compressed font
RETURN	accepts setup and displays options
M	selects Margin option
R	selects Right option
230	characters per line
RETURN	displays options
Q	selects Quit option and returns to main print menu
R	displays Range to print from
.	ellipsis - indicates from-to

Move cursor, with arrow keys, to last coordinate in area you wish to print. The screen will reverse to indicate the area being printed.

RETURN	executes the command
G	selects Go option and prints

To exit out of PRINT command, type:

Q	selects Quit option and exits out of PRINT command

LOADING YOUR WORKSHEET BACK INTO LOTUS 1-2-3

At a later date, when you need to use the worksheet to do further computations, just load your worksheet back into memory.

To do this, you must first clear memory if there is anything in it. To clear the memory,

Leave your cursor on any location and type:

/W	starts WORKSHEET command
E	selects Erase option
Y	Yes, to confirm

Now you are ready to load the worksheet into the memory, using 1-2-3's FILE command. To do this,

Place the data diskette from which you wish to load into Drive A.

Leave your cursor on any location and type:

/F	starts FILE command
R	selects Retrieve option

Place your cursor on the file name you wish to load, and press:

RETURN	executes the command

CHAPTER ELEVEN

EQUIVALENT YIELDS ON TAX-FREE AND TAXABLE BONDS

DESCRIPTION

In some areas municipal and state governments issue bonds which are tax-free. This means you do not have to pay federal income tax on the dividends which you receive. They do not pay a very high rate of interest, but many people feel that the income tax which they save results in a higher yield for them than some of the taxable investments. This exercise determines the equivalent tax yield on a tax free bond (Figures 1 and 2), and also the equivalent tax free yield on a taxable bond (Figures 3 and 4).

A Tax Free Bond (Figures 1 and 2)

EXAMPLE

An individual is considering buying a 6% tax-free yield municipal bond. She is in a 45% income tax bracket.

What taxable yield will she have to earn in order to receive the same amount after taxes?

SETTING UP YOUR WORKSHEET - ENTERING LABELS
(For Figure 1)

USE THE FOLLOWING STEP-BY-STEP DIRECTIONS FOR ENTERING THE LABELS IN FIGURE 1:

Enter your labels, in rows 1, 2 and 4, starting in A1 and continuing through A4, exactly as illustrated in Figure 1, retaining exact row and column locations of all information.

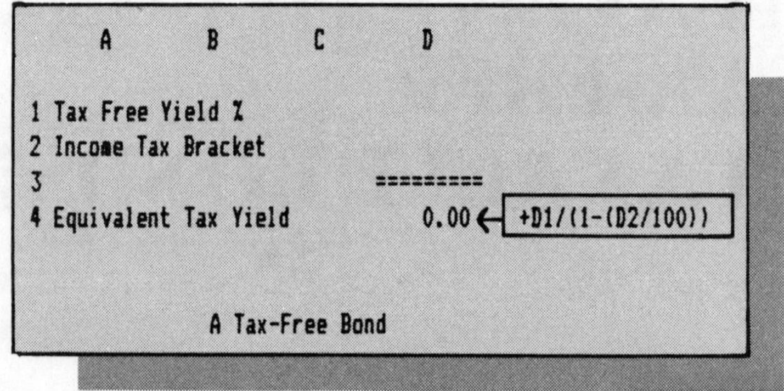

Figure 1

Next enter the double-dashed line in row 3.

Place your cursor on D3 and type:

\	starts REPEAT command
=	equal sign, label to be repeated
RETURN	executes the command

Now that you have entered your labels and the double-dashed line, you will enter the formula which will calculate the unknown value.

ENTERING THE FORMULA

USE THE FOLLOWING STEP-BY-STEP DIRECTIONS FOR ENTERING THE FORMULA
WHICH WILL CALCULATE THE UNKNOWN VALUE.

The formula, in column D, to the right of Equivalent Tax Yield, calculates the equivalent tax yield
you would have to earn to receive the same amount after taxes.

Place your cursor on D4 and type:

+ D 1 / (1 — (D 2 / 1 0 0))   formula

RETURN   enters the formula

You now need to format the coordinate into which you have just entered the formula so that it will
be displayed with two decimal places. To do this,

Leave your cursor on D4 and type:

/R   starts RANGE command

F   selects Format option

F   selects Fixed option and displays number of decimal
places: 2

RETURN   displays range to format: D4

RETURN   executes the command

Your worksheet should now look like Figure 1.

MAKING WORKSHEET ENTRIES

___ NOTE ___

Never enter values into coordinates containing formulas, or the
formulas will be erased.

Now that you have entered all the formulas, make your worksheet entries, above the double-dashed line, as illustrated in Figure 2.

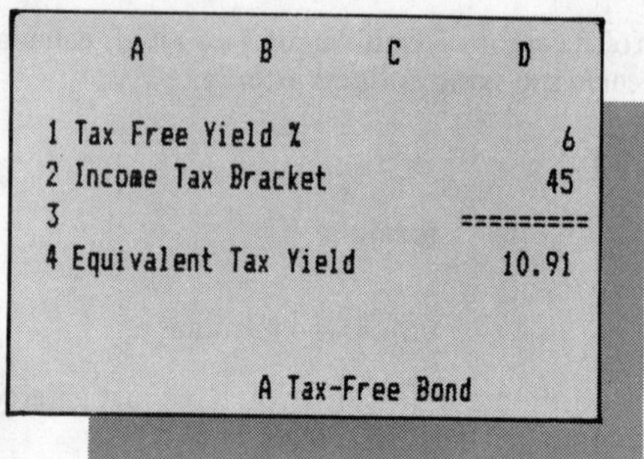

Figure 2

Now that your worksheet is complete, it is ready and all you need to do is enter your own set of known values.

SAVING YOUR WORKSHEET

Now save your worksheet for future use, so that the next time you wish to figure these computations all you will need to do is enter in your new known values, and you will not need to retype in the labels or enter the formulas.

To save your worksheet, place a formatted data diskette in Drive A.

With your cursor on any location, type:

/F   starts FILE command

S   selects Save option

Type in name of file.

RETURN   executes the command

PRINTING YOUR WORKSHEET

To print all or a portion of your worksheet, use the following directions, which are given for the Epson printer (compressed font).

Place your cursor on A1 and type:

/P	starts PRINT command
P	displays options
O	selects Options option
S	Selects Setup option and displays: Enter Setup String
\015	sets an Epson printer to compressed font
RETURN	accepts setup and displays options
M	selects Margin option
R	selects Right option
230	characters per line
RETURN	displays options
Q	selects Quit option and returns to main print menu
R	displays Range to print from
.	ellipsis - indicates from-to

Move cursor, with arrow keys, to last coordinate in area you wish to print. The screen will reverse to indicate the area being printed.

RETURN	executes the command
G	selects Go option and prints

To exit out of PRINT command, type:

Q	selects Quit option and exits out of PRINT command

Now you will clear the memory, in order to proceed with Figure 3 (A Taxable Bond). To do this:

Leave your cursor on any location and type:

/W	starts WORKSHEET command
E	selects Erase option
Y	Yes, to confirm

A Taxable Bond (Figures 3 and 4)

EXAMPLE

In the next exercise, assume that you currently own a taxable bond that pays 10% dividends. You are in a 38% income tax bracket.

What dividend rate will you need to earn in a tax-free bond to get the same return?

SETTING UP YOUR WORKSHEET - ENTERING LABELS (For Figure 3)

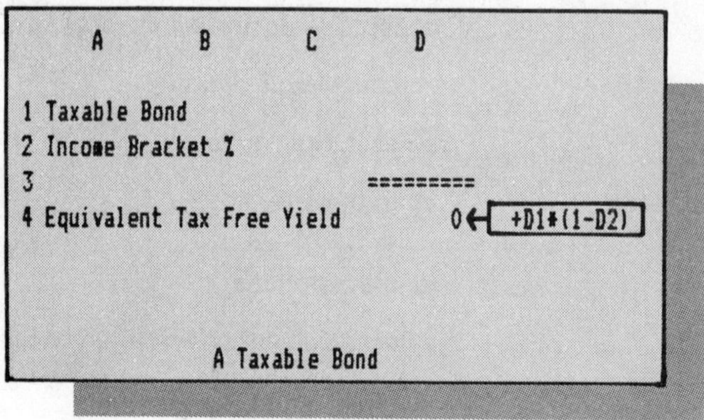

Figure 3

USE THE FOLLOWING STEP-BY-STEP DIRECTIONS FOR ENTERING THE LABELS IN FIGURE 3:

Enter your labels, starting in A1 and continuing through Row 4, exactly as illustrated in Figure 1, retaining exact row and column locations of all information.

Next enter the double-dashed line in row 3.

Place your cursor on D3 and type:

\	starts REPEAT command
=	equal sign, label to be repeated
RETURN	executes the command

Now that you have entered your labels and the double-dashed line, you will enter the formula which will calculate the unknown value.

ENTERING THE FORMULA

USE THE FOLLOWING STEP-BY-STEP DIRECTIONS FOR ENTERING THE FORMULA
WHICH WILL CALCULATE THE UNKNOWN VALUE.

The formula in column D, to the right of Equivalent Tax Free Yield, calculates the dividend rate
you need to earn in a tax-free bond to get the same return.

Place your cursor on D4 and type:

+ D 1 * (1 — D 2)   formula

RETURN   enters the formula

Now that you have entered the formula, your worksheet should look like Figure 3.

MAKING WORKSHEET ENTRIES

___ NOTE ___

Never enter values into coordinates containing formulas, or the
formulas will be erased.

Now that you have entered the formula, make your worksheet entries, in Column D, above the
double-dashed line, as illustrated in Figure 4.

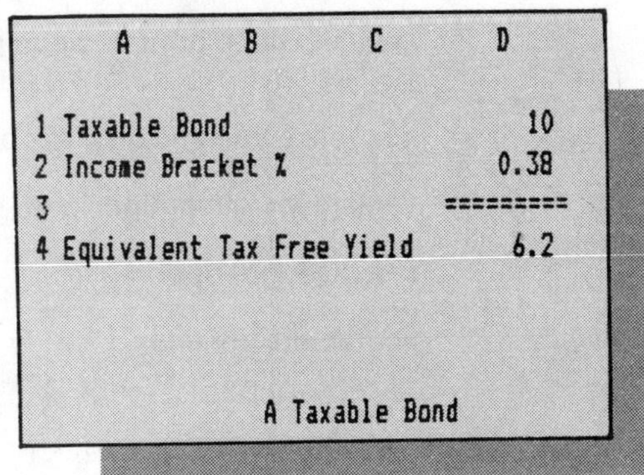

Figure 4

Now that your worksheet is complete, it is ready and all you need to do is enter your own set of known values.

SAVING YOUR WORKSHEET

Now save your worksheet for future use, so that the next time you wish to figure these computations all you will need to do is enter in your new known values, and you will not need to retype in the labels or enter the formulas.

To save your worksheet, place a formatted data diskette in Drive A.

With your cursor on any location, type:

/F	starts FILE command
S	selects Save option
Type in name of file.	
RETURN	executes the command

PRINTING YOUR WORKSHEET

To print all or a portion of your worksheet, use the following directions, which are given for the Epson printer (compressed font).

Place your cursor on A1 and type:

/P	starts PRINT command
P	displays options
O	selects Options option
S	Selects Setup option and displays: Enter Setup String
\015	sets an Epson printer to compressed font
RETURN	accepts setup and displays options
M	selects Margin option
R	selects Right option
230	characters per line
RETURN	displays options

Q	selects Quit option and returns to main print menu
R	displays Range to print from
.	ellipsis - indicates from-to

Move cursor, with arrow keys, to last coordinate in area you wish to print. The screen will reverse to indicate the area being printed.

RETURN	executes the command
G	selects Go option and prints

To exit out of PRINT command, type:

Q	selects Quit option and exits out of PRINT command

LOADING YOUR WORKSHEET BACK INTO LOTUS 1-2-3

At a later date, when you need to use the worksheet to do further computations, just load your worksheet back into memory.

To do this, you must first clear memory if there is anything in it. To clear the memory,

Leave your cursor on any location and type:

/W	starts WORKSHEET command
E	selects Erase option
Y	Yes, to confirm

Now you are ready to load the worksheet into the memory, using 1-2-3's FILE command. To do this,

Place the data diskette from which you wish to load into Drive A.

Leave your cursor on any location and type:

/F	starts FILE command
R	selects Retrieve option

Place your cursor on the file name you wish to load, and press:

RETURN	executes the command

CHAPTER TWELVE

WEIGHTED AVERAGE NUMBER OF SHARES

DESCRIPTION

When computing earnings per share, it is necessary to determine the weighted average number of shares outstanding during the period. In this exercise the weighted average number of shares outstanding is based on actual days held. Stock dividends and splits have not been considered.

EXAMPLE

The Maxwell Company entered 1976 with 50,000 shares, and ended that year with 59,300 shares.

On Jan. 25, 1976, 2500 shares were purchased, and the outstanding shares were 52,500.

On May 3, 1976, they purchased 8000 shares, which brought their outstanding shares to 60,500.

On Oct. 15, 1976, they sold 1200 shares, and then their outstanding shares were 59,300.

What was the weighted average number of shares outstanding during the 1976 period?

SETTING UP YOUR WORKSHEET - ENTERING LABELS

USE THE FOLLOWING STEP-BY-STEP DIRECTIONS FOR ENTERING THE LABELS IN
FIGURE 1:

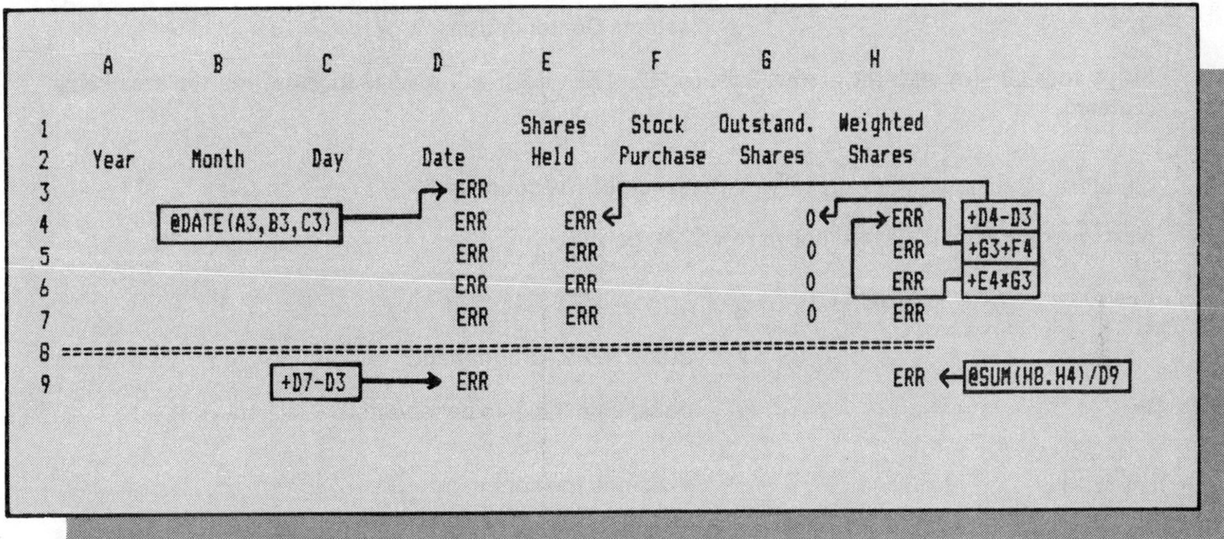

Figure 1

First you will expand all the columns to a width of 10 characters. To do this,

Leave your cursor on any location and type:

/W	starts WORKSHEET command
G	selects Global option
C	selects Column-width option
10	number of characters in column
RETURN	executes the command

Now enter the labels in rows 1 and 2, exactly as illustrated in Figure 1, retaining exact row and column locations of all information.

Next you will center the labels you have just entered in rows 1 and 2.

Place your cursor on A1 and type:

/R   starts RANGE command

L   selects Label option

C   selects Center option

Move your cursor, with the arrow keys, to H2. The screen will reverse to show you the area being centered.

RETURN   executes the command

Next enter the double-dashed line in row 8. To do this,

Place your cursor on A8 and type:

\   starts REPEAT command

=   equal sign, label to be repeated

RETURN   executes the command

The column your cursor is on will now have a line of dashes across its width. To extend the dashed line in the same row across the remaining columns,

Leave your cursor on A8 and type:

/C   starts COPY command and displays Range to copy from

RETURN   displays Range to copy to

B8   first coordinate to copy to

.   ellipsis - indicating from-to

H8   last coordinate to copy to

RETURN   executes the command

Now that you have entered your labels and the double-dashed line, you will begin entering the formulas which will calculate the unknown values.

ENTERING FORMULAS

USE THE FOLLOWING STEP-BY-STEP DIRECTIONS FOR ENTERING THE FORMULAS
WHICH WILL CALCULATE THE UNKNOWN VALUES.

Formula one, in the Date column, uses the Date function to generate an absolute number. Then that
number is formatted to display the day, month and year.

Place your cursor on D3 and type:

@DATE (A3 , B3 , C3)	formula
RETURN	enters the formula

Now format the coordinate into which you have just entered the formula, so that later in this exercise, when you enter the values into the Year, Month and Day columns, it will read in day, month
and year.

Leave your cursor on D3 and type:

/R	starts RANGE command
F	selects Format option
D	selects Date format
1	selects DD-MMM-YY, and displays Range to format
RETURN	executes the command

Now you will copy this formula, which has been formatted to read in day, month and year, down
the column.

Leave your cursor on D3 and type:

/C	starts COPY command and displays Range to copy from: D3
RETURN	displays Range to copy to
D4	first coordinate to copy to
.	ellipsis - indicates from-to
D7	last coordinate to copy to
RETURN	executes the command

Formula two, in the Shares Held column, calculates the number of days the shares are held.

Place your cursor on E4 and type:

+ D4 — D3   formula

RETURN   executes the command

Now you will copy formula two down the column.

Leave your cursor on E4 and type:

/C   starts COPY command and displays Range to copy from

RETURN   displays Range to copy to

E5   first coordinate to copy to

.   ellipsis - indicates from-to

E7   last coordinate to copy to

RETURN   executes the command

Formula three, in the Outstanding Shares column, calculates the number of shares held after each transaction.

Place your cursor on G4 and type:

+ G 3 + F 4   formula

RETURN   enters the formula

Formula four, in the Weighted Shares column, calculates the weighted shares.

Place your cursor on H4 and type:

+ E 4 * G 3   formula

RETURN   enters the formula

Now you will copy formulas three and four, which you have just entered, down their respective columns.

Place your cursor on G4 and type:

/C   starts COPY command and displays Range to copy from: G4

Move your cursor, with the arrow keys, to H4. The screen will reverse to show you which coordinates are being copied.

`RETURN`	displays Range to copy to
	ellipsis - indicates from-to

Move your cursor to G7, with the arrow keys. The screen will reverse to show you which coordinates are being copied into.

`RETURN`	executes the command

Formula five, beneath the double-dashed line, in the Date column, calculates the total number of days during which all the transactions took place.

Place your cursor on D9 and type:

+ D 7 — D 3	formula
`RETURN`	executes the command

Formula six, beneath the double-dashed line, in the Weighted Shares column, calculates the weighted average number of shares outstanding during the year.

Place your cursor on H9 and type:

@SUM (H 8 . H 4) / D 9	formula
`RETURN`	enters the formula

Now you will format the coordinate into which you have just entered the formula so that it will be displayed with two decimal places.

Leave your cursor on H9 and type:

/R	starts RANGE command
F	selects Format option
F	selects Fixed option and displays number of decimal places: 2
`RETURN`	displays Range to format: H9
`RETURN`	executes the command

Now that you have entered all the formulas, your worksheet should look like Figure 1.

MAKING WORKSHEET ENTRIES

NOTE

Never enter values into coordinates containing formulas, or the formulas will be erased.

Now that you have entered all the formulas, make your worksheet entries, as illustrated in Figure 2, above the double-dashed line, using the following instructions:

	A	B	C	D	E	F	G	H
1					Shares	Stock	Outstand.	Weighted
2	Year	Month	Day	Date	Held	Purchase	Shares	Shares
3	76	1	1	01-Jan-76			50000	
4	76	1	25	25-Jan-76	24	2500	52500	1200000
5	76	5	3	03-May-76	99	8000	60500	5197500
6	76	10	15	15-Oct-76	165	-1200	59300	9982500
7	76	12	31	31-Dec-76	77	0	59300	4566100
8	==
9				365				57386.58

Figure 2

Enter the values in the Year column, beginning in coordinate A3, until you reach the double-dashed line.

Next enter the values in the Month and Day columns, beginning again in row 3, until you reach the double-dashed line.

Next enter the values in the Stock Purchase column, BEGINNING WITH ROW 4, until you reach the double-dashed line.

Last, enter the value (50000), which is the number of outstanding shares at the beginning of the year, in the Outstanding Shares column, in ROW 3 ONLY.

Now that your worksheet is complete, it is ready and all you need to do is enter your own set of known values.

SAVING YOUR WORKSHEET

Now save your worksheet for future use, so that the next time you wish to figure these computations all you will need to do is enter in your new known values, and you will not need to retype in the labels or enter the formulas.

To save your worksheet, place a formatted data diskette in Drive A.

With your cursor on any location, type:

/F	starts FILE command
S	selects Save option

Type in name of file.

RETURN	executes the command

PRINTING YOUR WORKSHEET

To print all or a portion of your worksheet, use the following directions, which are given for the Epson printer (compressed font).

Place your cursor on A1 and type:

/P	starts PRINT command
P	displays options
O	selects Options option
S	Selects Setup option and displays: Enter Setup String
\ 015	sets an Epson printer to compressed font
RETURN	accepts setup and displays options
M	selects Margin option
R	selects Right option
230	characters per line
RETURN	displays options
Q	selects Quit option and returns to main print menu
R	displays Range to print from
.	ellipsis - indicates from-to

Move cursor, with arrow keys, to last coordinate in area you wish to print. The screen will reverse to indicate the area being printed.

| RETURN | executes the command |

G   selects Go option and prints

To exit out of PRINT command, type:

Q   selects Quit option and exits out of PRINT command

LOADING YOUR WORKSHEET BACK INTO LOTUS 1-2-3

At a later date, when you need to use the worksheet to do further computations, just load your worksheet back into memory.

To do this, you must first clear memory if there is anything in it. To clear the memory,

Leave your cursor on any location and type:

/W   starts WORKSHEET command

E   selects Erase option

Y   Yes, to confirm

Now you are ready to load the worksheet into the memory, using 1-2-3's FILE command. To do this,

Place the data diskette from which you wish to load into Drive A.

Leave your cursor on any location and type:

/F   starts FILE command

R   selects Retrieve option

Place your cursor on the file name you wish to load, and press:

| RETURN | executes the command |

CHAPTER THIRTEEN

COMPUTATIONS FOR TREASURY BILLS

COMPUTATION OF BANK DISCOUNT

DESCRIPTION

Although Treasury bills are widely quoted and traded on a rate basis often called "yield," they are actually quoted and figured on a bank discount basis and many factors must be considered when computing their yield. It is necessary to determine the investment yield on a per annum basis, the investment yield per hundred dollars invested, as well as converting the discount basis to the approximate investment yield.

EXAMPLE

Mr. Andrew Watson is examining a particular Treasury bill which has a dollar price of $91.85 after full discount. The number of days per year used is 360, the discount basis is 8.46% and the days to maturity is 347.

He needs to determine the yield of this bill based on the yield on a per annum basis, the yield per hundred dollars invested, and he will also want to convert the discount basis to the approximate investment yield.

SETTING UP YOUR WORKSHEET - ENTERING LABELS for Figure 1)

USE THE FOLLOWING STEP-BY-STEP DIRECTIONS FOR ENTERING THE LABELS IN FIGURE 1:

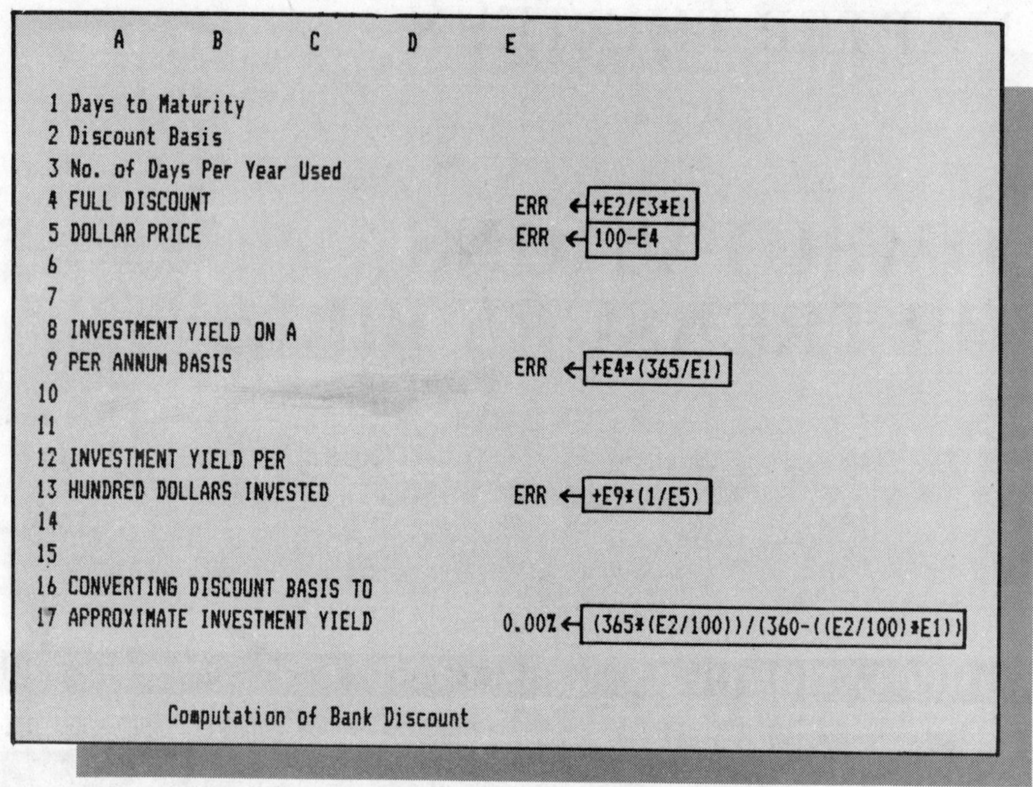

Figure 1

Enter your labels, starting in A1 and continuing through A17, exactly as illustrated in Figure 1, retaining exact row and column locations of all information.

Now that you have entered your labels, you will begin entering the formulas which will calculate the unknown values.

ENTERING FORMULAS

USE THE FOLLOWING STEP-BY-STEP DIRECTIONS FOR ENTERING THE FORMULAS WHICH WILL CALCULATE THE UNKNOWN VALUES.

Formula one, in column E, will determine the full discount per $100 maturity value for a Treasury bill due in 347 days on an 8.46 percent discount basis, based on 360 days per year.

Place your cursor on E4 and type:

+ E 2 / E 3 * E 1   formula

RETURN   enters the formula

Formula two, in column E, will determine the dollar price for that Treasury bill.

Place your cursor on E5 and type:

100-E4   formula

RETURN   enters the formula

Formula three, in column E, determines the investment yield on a per annum basis. The investment return or yield on a Treasury bill is at a higher rate than the discount basis. In this computation the discount is based on 365 days.

Place your cursor on E9 and type:

+ E 4 * (3 6 5 / E 1)   formula

RETURN   enters the formula

Formula four, in column E, determines the investment yield per annum (percentage) per hundred dollars invested.

Place your cursor on E13 and type:

+ E 9 * (1 / E 5)   formula

RETURN   enters the formula

Formula five, in column E, determines the investment return or yield when converting discount basis to approximate investment yield.

Place your cursor on E17 and type:

(3 6 5 * (E 2 / 1 0 0)) / (3 6 0 — ((E 2 / 1 0 0) * E 1))   formula

RETURN   enters the formula

Now that the formulas are entered, you will format some of the coordinates. E5 and E9 need to be formatted to be displayed in Currency. To do this,

Place your cursor on E5 and type:

/ R	starts RANGE command
F	selects Format option
C	selects Currency option
4	number of decimal places
RETURN	displays range to format

Move your cursor to E9 with the arrow key. The screen will reverse to show which coordinates are being formatted.

| RETURN | executes the command |

Coordinates E13 and E17 need to be formatted to be displayed in Percentage. To do this,

Place your cursor on E13 and type:

/R	starts RANGE command
F	selects Format option
P	selects Percent option
2	number of decimal places
RETURN	displays range to format

Move your cursor to E17 with the arrow keys. Note the screen will reverse to show the area being formatted.

| RETURN | executes the command |

Your worksheet should now look like Figure 1.

MAKING WORKSHEET ENTRIES

______ **NOTE** ______

Never enter values into coordinates containing formulas, or the formulas will be erased.

Now that you have entered all the formulas, make your worksheet entries, into column E, Row 1 (Days To Maturity), Row 2 (Discount Basis) and Row 3 (No. of Days Per Year Used), as illustrated in Figure 2.

```
          A        B      C      D        E

 1 Days to Maturity                      347
 2 Discount Basis                        8.46
 3 No. of Days Per Year Used             360
 4 FULL DISCOUNT                         8.1545
 5 DOLLAR PRICE                        $91.8455
 6
 7
 8 INVESTMENT YIELD ON A
 9 PER ANNUM BASIS                      $8.5775
10
11
12 INVESTMENT YIELD PER
13 HUNDRED DOLLARS INVESTED              9.34%
14
15
16 CONVERTING DISCOUNT BASIS TO
17 APPROXIMATE INVESTMENT YIELD          9.34%


          Computation of Bank Discount
```

Figure 2

Now that your worksheet is complete, it is ready and all you need to do is enter your own set of known values.

SAVING YOUR WORKSHEET

Now save your worksheet for future use, so that the next time you wish to figure these computations all you will need to do is enter in your new known values, and you will not need to retype in the labels or enter the formulas.

To save your worksheet, place a formatted data diskette in Drive A.

With your cursor on any location, type:

/F	starts FILE command
S	selects Save option

Type in name of file.

RETURN	executes the command

PRINTING YOUR WORKSHEET

To print all or a portion of your worksheet, use the following directions, which are given for the Epson printer (compressed font).

Place your cursor on A1 and type:

/P	starts PRINT command
P	displays options
O	selects Options option
S	Selects Setup option and displays: Enter Setup String
\ 015	sets an Epson printer to compressed font
RETURN	accepts setup and displays options
M	selects Margin option
R	selects Right option
230	characters per line
RETURN	displays options
Q	selects Quit option and returns to main print menu
R	displays Range to print from
.	ellipsis - indicates from-to

Move cursor, with arrow keys, to last coordinate in area you wish to print. The screen will reverse to indicate the area being printed.

RETURN	accepts range to be printed

| G | selects Go option and prints |

To exit out of PRINT command, type:

| Q | selects Quit option and exits out of PRINT command |

To continue on to Figure 3, first clear the memory.

Leave your cursor on any location and type:

/W	starts WORKSHEET command
E	selects Erase option
Y	Yes, to confirm

TREASURY BILL RETURNS (Figure 3)

U.S. Treasury bills are frequently sold prior to maturity at a rate basis different from that at which they were purchased. Investors may desire to determine the return from bills under such conditions, or how long bills need to be held to avoid loss. The following formulas can be used for those calculations in most situations. For extreme accuracy, where large amounts are involved, the investor should refer to the computation tables and formulas issued by the Treasury Department in Circular No. 300, Fourth Revision.

EXAMPLE

Mr. Watson now wants to examine another type of treasury bill. He knows the number of days to maturity (347), the original rate of discount (8.46), the number of days held (45), and the difference between the rate at which bills are purchased and that at which they are sold (40%).

He needs to determine the alteration in the original cost resulting from the difference between the purchase price and the sale price over the period held. He also needs to know the return for the period held, and at what rate the bills must be sold.

SETTING UP YOUR WORKSHEET - ENTERING LABELS (For Figure 3)

USE THE FOLLOWING STEP-BY-STEP DIRECTIONS FOR ENTERING THE LABELS IN FIGURE 3:

Enter your labels, starting in A1 and continuing through A22, exactly as illustrated in Figure 3, retaining exact row and column locations of all information.

Now that you have entered your labels, you will begin entering the formulas which will calculate the unknown values.

A   B   C   D   E   F   G
1 Number of Days to Maturity of
2 Treasury Bills When Purchased
3
4 Original Rate of Discount
5
6 Number of Days Held
7
8 Difference Between the Rate at Which
9 Bills are Purchased and That at Which
10 They Are Sold
11
12 ALTERATION IN ORIGINAL COST (RATE) RESULTING
13 FROM DIFFERENCE BETWEEN PURCHASE PRICE AND
14 SALE PRICE OVER PERIOD HELD   ERR ← (G2-G6)/G6*G10
15
16
17
18 RETURN FOR PERIOD HELD   ERR ← G4+G14
19
20
21
22 THEREFORE, BILLS MUST BE SOLD AT   0 ← +G4-G10

Treasury Bill Returns

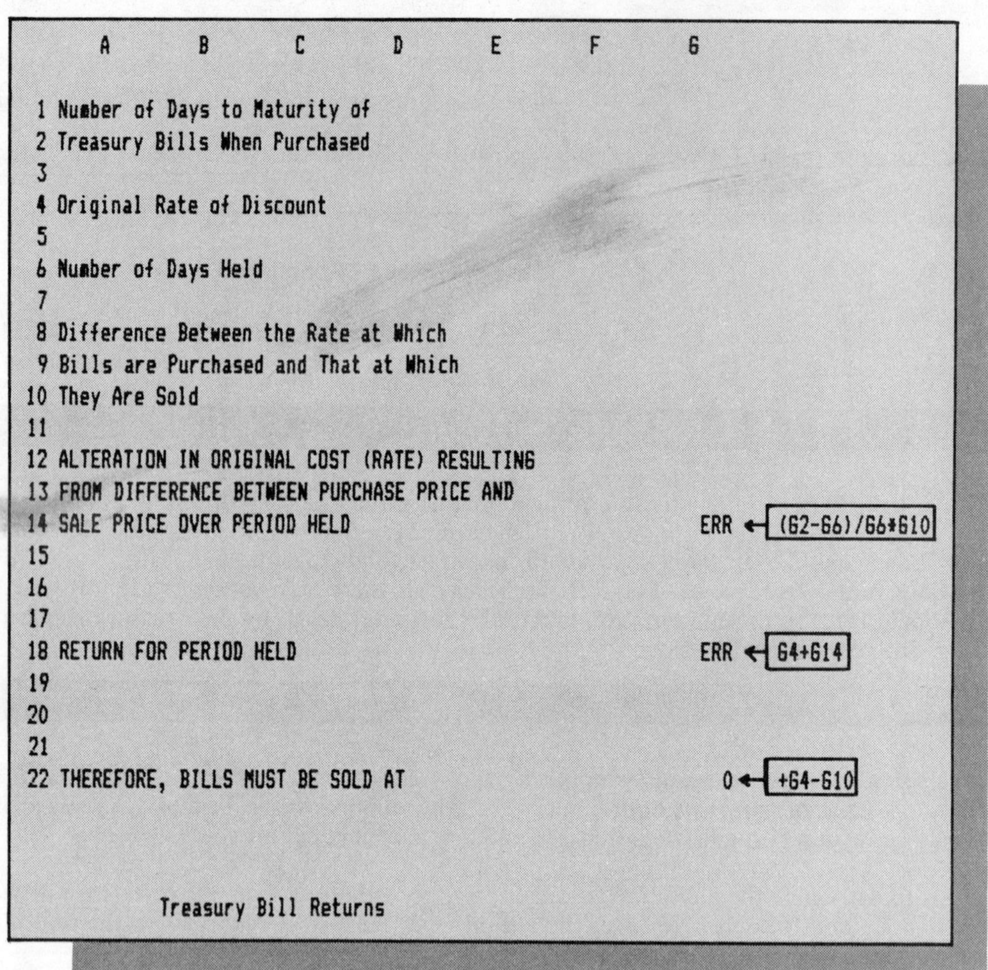

Figure 3

ENTERING FORMULAS

USE THE FOLLOWING STEP-BY-STEP DIRECTIONS FOR ENTERING THE FORMULAS
WHICH WILL CALCULATE THE UNKNOWN VALUES.

Formula one, in column G, shows how original rate of 8.46% was altered by 2.6844%. Since bills
were sold at a rate basis lower than the cost, representing a gain, the original rate was increased and
the figure of 2.6844% represents an addition.

Place your cursor on G14 and type:

(G 2 — G 6) / G 6 * G 1 0   formula

[RETURN]   enters the formula

Formula two, in column G, adds original rate (8.46) to alteration (2.6844) and arrives at return for
period held.

Place your cursor on G18 and type:

+ G 4 + G 1 4   formula

[RETURN]   enters the formula

Formula three, in column G, shows the difference between purchase price and sale price necessary
to show a return of 10.4733 percent, and illustrates that the bills must be sold at 8.46% minus .40%,
or 8.06%.

Place your cursor on G22 and type:

+ G 4 — G 1 0   formula

[RETURN]   enters the formula

Your worksheet should now look like Figure 3.

MAKING WORKSHEET ENTRIES

NOTE

Never enter values into coordinates containing formulas, or the
formulas will be erased.

Now that you have entered all the formulas, make your worksheet entries into Rows 2, 4, 6 and 10,
as illustrated in Figure 4.

Now that your worksheet is complete, it is ready and all you need to do is enter your own set of
known values.

```
            A      B      C      D      E      F      G

 1 Number of Days to Maturity of
 2 Treasury Bills When Purchased                        347

 3
 4 Original Rate of Discount                            8.46
 5
 6 Number of Days Held                                   45
 7
 8 Difference Between the Rate at Which
 9 Bills are Purchased and That at Which
10 They Are Sold                                         0.4
11
12 ALTERATION IN ORIGINAL COST (RATE) RESULTING
13 FROM DIFFERENCE BETWEEN PURCHASE PRICE AND
14 SALE PRICE OVER PERIOD HELD                         2.6844
15
16
17
18 RETURN FOR PERIOD HELD                             11.1444
19
20
21
22 THEREFORE, BILLS MUST BE SOLD AT                    8.06



                 Treasury Bill Returns
```

Figure 4

SAVING YOUR WORKSHEET

Now save your worksheet for future use, so that the next time you wish to figure these computations all you will need to do is enter in your new known values, and you will not need to retype in the labels or enter the formulas.

To save your worksheet, place a formatted data diskette in Drive A.

With your cursor on any location, type:

/F	starts FILE command
S	selects Save option

Type in name of file.

RETURN	executes the command

PRINTING YOUR WORKSHEET

To print all or a portion of your worksheet, use the following directions, which are given for the Epson printer (compressed font).

Place your cursor on A1 and type:

/P	starts PRINT command
P	displays options
O	selects Options option
S	Selects Setup option and displays: Enter Setup String
\015	sets an Epson printer to compressed font
RETURN	accepts setup and displays options
M	selects Margin option
R	selects Right option
230	characters per line
RETURN	displays options

Q	selects Quit option and returns to main print menu
R	displays Range to print from
.	ellipsis - indicates from-to

Move cursor, with arrow keys, to last coordinate in area you wish to print. The screen will reverse to indicate the area being printed.

RETURN	accepts range to be printed
G	selects Go option and prints

To exit out of PRINT command, type:

Q	selects Quit option and exits out of PRINT command

LOADING YOUR WORKSHEET BACK INTO LOTUS 1-2-3

At a later date, when you need to use the worksheet to do further computations, just load your worksheet back into memory.

To do this, you must first clear memory if there is anything in it. To clear the memory,

Leave your cursor on any location and type:

/W	starts WORKSHEET command
E	selects Erase option
Y	Yes, to confirm

Now you are ready to load the worksheet into the memory, using 1-2-3's FILE command. To do this,

Place the data diskette from which you wish to load into Drive A.

Leave your cursor on any location and type:

/F	starts FILE command
R	selects Retrieve option

Place your cursor on the file name you wish to load, and press:

RETURN	executes the command

CHAPTER FOURTEEN

COMPUTATION OF REBATE DUE

DESCRIPTION

When a borrower considers paying off a loan before the end of its original life, he wants to know how much of an interest rebate he will receive, and how much money he will need in order to pay off the loan. The "Rule of 78's" is a formula commonly used in calculating rebate due. Once the rebate due is determined, it is easy to find the payoff amount.

Finding the payoff amount is solved in this exercise in three stages: First the total interest due on the original loan is calculated. Second, using the Rule of 78's, the rebate received for early payoff is computed. Finally, the payoff amount is determined by multiplying the number of payments left by the payment amount, and then subtracting the rebate. The answer is the amount of the payoff.

EXAMPLE

After making 18 payments on his three-year (36 month) car loan, a borrower is contemplating paying off his three-year (36 month) car loan. He originally borrowed $5000 at 5% add-on annual interest, and his monthly payments are $159.72.

If he pays off his loan, how much interest will be rebated, and what amount will pay off his loan?

SETTING UP YOUR WORKSHEET - ENTERING LABELS

USE THE FOLLOWING STEP-BY-STEP DIRECTIONS FOR ENTERING THE LABELS IN FIGURE 1:

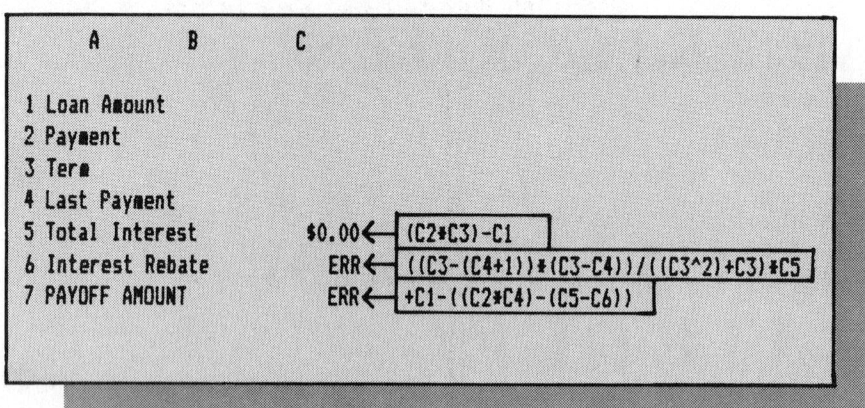

Figure 1

First, column C needs to be expanded to allow for 12 characters.

Place your cursor on column C and type:

/W	starts WORKSHEET command
C	selects Column-Width option
S	selects Set option
12	number of spaces in column
RETURN	executes the command

You will now format some of the coordinates so that later, when values and formulas are entered, they will be displayed in currency. To do this,

Place your cursor on C1 and type:

/R	starts RANGE command
F	selects Format option
C	selects Currency option and displays decimal places: 2
[RETURN]	displays range to format: C1

Move cursor, with arrow keys, to C2. The screen will reverse to show the area being formatted.

[RETURN]	executes the command

Now place your cursor on C5 and type:

/R	starts RANGE command
F	selects Format option
C	selects Currency option and displays decimal places: 2
[RETURN]	displays range to format: C5

Move cursor, with arrow keys, to C7. The screen will reverse to show the area being formatted.

[RETURN]	executes the command

Now enter your labels, starting in A1, and continuing through A7, exactly as illustrated in Figure 1, retaining exact row and column locations of all information.

Now that you have entered your labels, you will begin entering the formulas which will calculate the unknown values.

ENTERING FORMULAS

USE THE FOLLOWING STEP-BY-STEP DIRECTIONS FOR ENTERING THE FORMULAS WHICH WILL CALCULATE THE UNKNOWN VALUES.

Formula one, in column C, to the right of Total Interest, will calculate the total interest due on the original loan.

Place your cursor on C5 and type:

(C 2 * C 3) — C 1	formula
[RETURN]	enters the formula

Formula two, in column C, to the right of Interest Rebate, calculates the rebate received for early payoff.

Place your cursor on C6 and type:

$((C3-(C4+1))*(C3-C4))/((C3\char94 2)+C3)*C5$ formula

RETURN   enters the formula

Formula three, in column C, to the right of PAYOFF AMOUNT, multiplies the number of payments left by the payment, and then subtracts the rebate, to determine the Payoff Amount.

Place your cursor on C7 and type:

$+C1-((C2*C4)-(C5-C6))$ formula

RETURN   enters the formula

Your worksheet should now look like Figure 1.

MAKING WORKSHEET ENTRIES

NOTE

Never enter values into coordinates containing formulas, or the formulas will be erased.

Now that you have entered all the formulas, make your worksheet entries, in Column C, in Rows 1, 2, 3 and 4, as illustrated in Figure 2.

Now that your worksheet is complete, it is ready and all you need to do is enter your own set of known values.

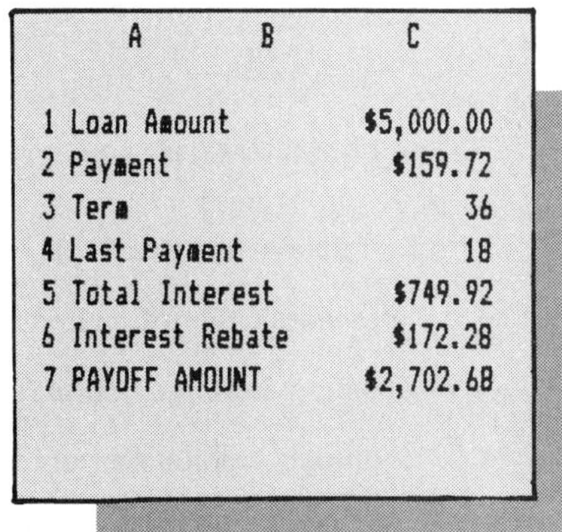

Figure 2

SAVING YOUR WORKSHEET

Now save your worksheet for future use, so that the next time you wish to figure these computations all you will need to do is enter in your new known values, and you will not need to retype in the labels or enter the formulas.

To save your worksheet, place a formatted data diskette in Drive A.

With your cursor on any location, type:

/F	starts FILE command
S	selects Save option

Type in name of file.

RETURN	executes the command

PRINTING YOUR WORKSHEET

To print all or a portion of your worksheet, use the following directions, which are given for the Epson printer (compressed font).

Place your cursor on A1 and type:

/P	starts PRINT command
P	displays options
O	selects Options option
S	Selects Setup option and displays: Enter Setup String
\015	sets an Epson printer to compressed font
RETURN	accepts setup and displays options

M	selects Margin option
R	selects Right option
230	characters per line
RETURN	displays options
Q	selects Quit option and returns to main print menu
R	displays Range to print from
.	ellipsis - indicates from-to

Move cursor, with arrow keys, to last coordinate in area you wish to print. The screen will reverse to indicate the area being printed.

| RETURN | executes the command |
| G | selects Go option and prints |

To exit out of PRINT command, type:

| Q | selects Quit option and exits out of PRINT command |

LOADING YOUR WORKSHEET BACK INTO LOTUS 1-2-3

At a later date, when you need to use the worksheet to do further computations, just load your worksheet back into memory.

To do this, you must first clear memory if there is anything in it. To clear the memory,

Leave your cursor on any location and type:

/W	starts WORKSHEET command
E	selects Erase option
Y	Yes, to confirm

Now you are ready to load the worksheet into the memory, using 1-2-3's FILE command. To do this,

Place the data diskette from which you wish to load into Drive A.

Leave your cursor on any location and type:

| /F | starts FILE command |
| R | selects Retrieve option |

Place your cursor on the file name you wish to load, and press:

| RETURN | executes the command |

CHAPTER FIFTEEN

CAPITAL ASSET PRICING MODEL

DESCRIPTION

This pricing model is used to derive the expected future return on a security.

EXAMPLE

An analyst is examining a particular security. He knows the risk-free rate of interest, the expected return on the market portfolio of securities, and the volatility of stock return, i.e., the degree of responsiveness relative to that of the market portfolio.

He wants to determine the expected future return on the security for the coming period.

SETTING UP YOUR WORKSHEET - ENTERING LABELS

Enter your labels, starting in A1 and continuing through A10, exactly as illustrated in Figure 1, retaining exact row and column locations of all information.

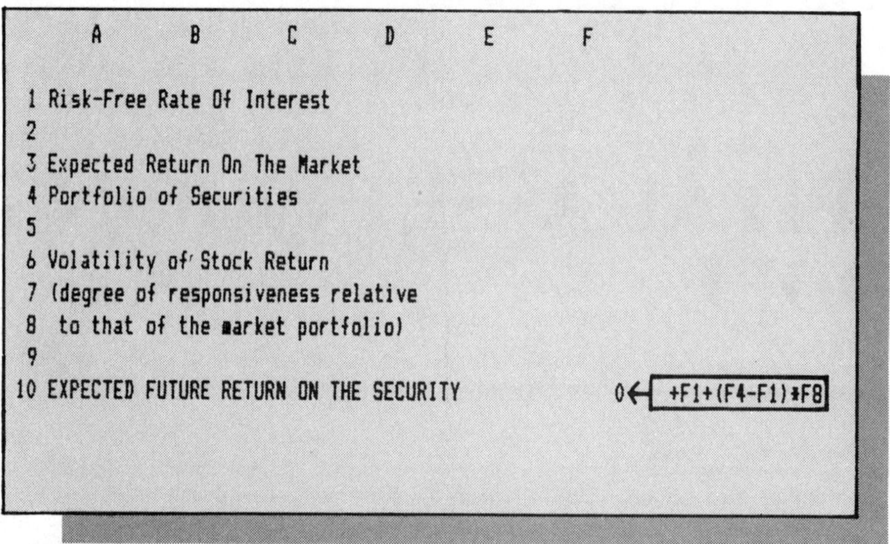

Figure 1

Now that you have entered your labels, you will enter the formula which will calculate the unknown value.

ENTERING THE FORMULA

USE THE FOLLOWING STEP-BY-STEP DIRECTIONS FOR ENTERING THE FORMULA WHICH WILL CALCULATE THE UNKNOWN VALUE.

To enter the formula into column F, which will calculate the Expected Future Return On The Security,

Place your cursor on F10 and type:

+ F 1 + (F 4 — F 1) * F 8   formula

RETURN   enters the formula

Your worksheet should now look like Figure 1.

MAKING WORKSHEET ENTRIES

NOTE

Never enter values into coordinates containing formulas, or the formulas will be erased.

Now that you have entered all the formulas, make your worksheet entries, into column F, Rows 1, 4 and 8, as illustrated in Figure 2.

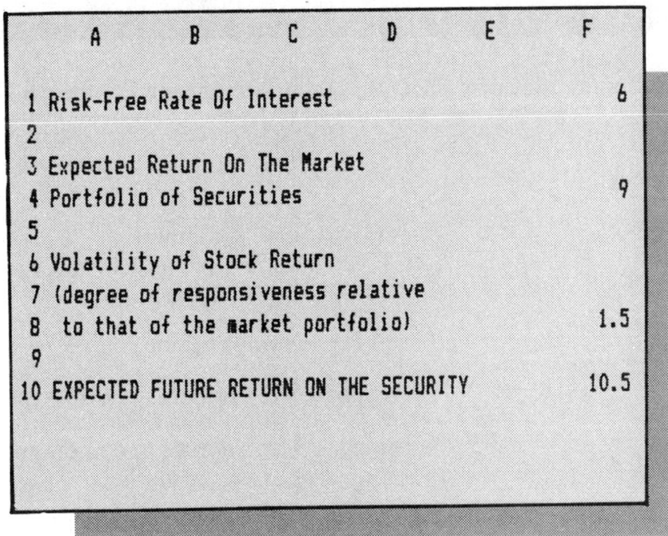

Figure 2

Now that your worksheet is complete, it is ready and all you need to do is enter your own set of known values.

SAVING YOUR WORKSHEET

Now save your worksheet for future use, so that the next time you wish to figure these computations all you will need to do is enter in your new known values, and you will not need to retype in the labels or enter the formulas.

To save your worksheet, place a formatted data diskette in Drive A.

With your cursor on any location, type:

/F	starts FILE command
S	selects Save option

Type in name of file.

RETURN	executes the command

PRINTING YOUR WORKSHEET

To print all or a portion of your worksheet, use the following directions, which are given for the Epson printer (compressed font).

Place your cursor on A1 and type:

/P	starts PRINT command
P	displays options
O	selects Options option
S	Selects Setup option and displays: Enter Setup String
\015	sets an Epson printer to compressed font
RETURN	accepts setup and displays options
M	selects Margin option
R	selects Right option
230	characters per line
RETURN	displays options

Q	selects Quit option and returns to main print menu
R	displays Range to print from
.	ellipsis - indicates from-to

Move cursor, with arrow keys, to last coordinate in area you wish to print. The screen will reverse to indicate the area being printed.

`RETURN`	executes the command
G	selects Go option and prints

To exit out of PRINT command, type:

Q	selects Quit option and exits out of PRINT command

LOADING YOUR WORKSHEET BACK INTO LOTUS 1-2-3

At a later date, when you need to use the worksheet to do further computations, just load your worksheet back into memory.

To do this, you must first clear memory if there is anything in it. To clear the memory,

Leave your cursor on any location and type:

/W	starts WORKSHEET command
E	selects Erase option
Y	Yes, to confirm

Now you are ready to load the worksheet into the memory, using 1-2-3's FILE command. To do this,

Place the data diskette from which you wish to load into Drive A.

Leave your cursor on any location and type:

/F	starts FILE command
R	selects Retrieve option

Place your cursor on the file name you wish to load, and press:

`RETURN`	executes the command

CHAPTER SIXTEEN

A CASH MANAGEMENT MODEL

DESCRIPTION

When a company is charged for a transfer of money from their cash account to an investment account, two factors need to be determined:

1) The point to which the balance is returned.

2) Upper allowable limit for the cash balance (When should cash be transferred into the investment account?)

This cash management model, developed by Miller and Orr (see reference at end of book) minimizes the total of the expected cost of transfers between the investment and the cash accounts of a company, along with the opportunity cost of holding cash.

EXAMPLE

In this exercise, a company is being charged $30 to transfer money between its cash and investment accounts. The variance of the daily changes in the cash balance is $200,000. The interest rate on its investment account is 9% annually, compounded daily.

What is the return point for the cash account, and what is the upper allowable limit for the cash balance?

If a positive minimum cash level is required in the account (for example, if a minimum of $5000 is required in the account), what would the return point become?

SETTING UP YOUR WORKSHEET - ENTERING LABELS

USE THE FOLLOWING STEP-BY-STEP DIRECTIONS FOR ENTERING THE LABELS IN FIGURE 1:

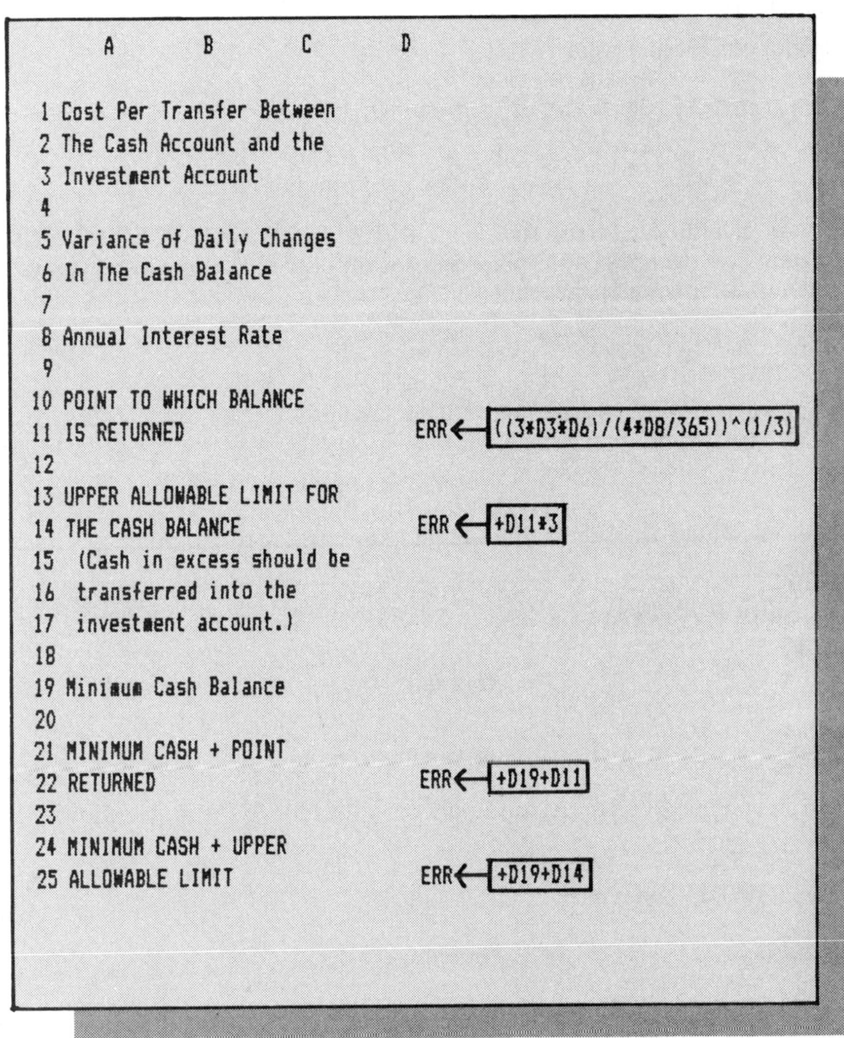

Figure 1

Enter your labels, starting in A1, and continuing through A25, exactly as illustrated in Figure 1, retaining exact row and column locations of all information.

Now that you have entered your labels you will begin entering the formulas which will calculate the unknown values.

ENTERING FORMULAS

USE THE FOLLOWING STEP-BY-STEP DIRECTIONS FOR ENTERING THE FORMULAS WHICH WILL CALCULATE THE UNKNOWN VALUES.

Formula one, in column D, to the right of POINT TO WHICH BALANCE IS RETURNED, computes a return point to which the cash balance is returned if cash is either transferred into the investment account or obtained from the investment account. (When the cash balance hits zero, cash in the amount of this return point is transferred from the investment). To enter the formula,

Place your cursor on D11 and type:

((3 * D 3 * D 6) / (4 * D 8 / 365)) ^ (1 / 3)   formula

RETURN   enters the formula

Formula two, in column D, to the right of UPPER ALLOWABLE LIMIT FOR THE CASH BALANCE, computes the upper allowable limit for the cash balance. (Cash in excess of this should be transferred into the investment account.)

Place your cursor on D14 and type:

+ D 1 1 * 3   formula

RETURN   enters the formula

Formula three, in column D, adds the minimum cash balance to the point to which the balance is returned.

Place your cursor on D22 and type:

+ D 1 9 + D 1 1   formula

RETURN   enters the formula

Formula four, in column D, adds the minimum cash balance to the upper allowable limit for cash balance.

Place your cursor on D25 and type:

+ D 1 9 + D 1 4   formula

RETURN   enters the formula

Now you will format some of the coordinates into which you have entered formulas so that later they will be displayed with two decimal places.

Place your cursor on D11 and type:

/R	starts RANGE command
F	selects Format option
F	selects Fixed option and displays number of decimal places: 2
[RETURN]	displays Range to format: D11

Move your cursor, with arrow keys, to D14. Screen will reverse to show area being formatted.

[RETURN]	executes the command

Place your cursor on D22 and type:

/R	starts RANGE command
F	selects Format option
F	selects Fixed option and displays number of decimal places: 2
[RETURN]	displays Range to format: D22
[RETURN]	executes the command

Your worksheet should now look like Figure 1.

MAKING WORKSHEET ENTRIES

___ **NOTE** ___

Never enter values into coordinates containing formulas, or the formulas will be erased.

Now that you have entered all the formulas, make your worksheet entries, in column D, in rows 3, 6, 8, and 19, as illustrated in Figure 2.

```
              A      B      C      D

   1 Cost Per Transfer Between
   2 The Cash Account and the
   3 Investment Account          30
   4
   5 Variance of Daily Changes
   6 In The Cash Balance         200000
   7
   8 Annual Interest Rate        0.09
   9
  10 POINT TO WHICH BALANCE
  11 IS RETURNED                 2632.82
  12
  13 UPPER ALLOWABLE LIMIT FOR
  14 THE CASH BALANCE            7898.46
  15  (Cash in excess should be
  16  transferred into the
  17  investment account.)
  18
  19 Minimum Cash Balance        5000
  20
  21 MINIMUM CASH + POINT
  22 RETURNED                    7632.82
  23
  24 MINIMUM CASH + UPPER
  25 ALLOWABLE LIMIT             12898.45
```

Figure 2

Do not forget to enter the value in row 19, the Minimum Cash Balance. In this exercise, the bank requires that a positive minimum cash level of $5,000 be kept in the account. Therefore, that amount will be added to both the Point To Which The Balance is Returned and The Upper Allowable Limit For Cash Balance.

Now that your worksheet is complete, it is ready and all you need to do is enter your own set of known values.

SAVING YOUR WORKSHEET

Now save your worksheet for future use, so that the next time you wish to figure these computations all you will need to do is enter in your new known values, and you will not need to retype in the labels or enter the formulas.

To save your worksheet, place a formatted data diskette in Drive A.

With your cursor on any location, type:

/F	starts FILE command
S	selects Save option

Type in name of file.

RETURN	executes the command

PRINTING YOUR WORKSHEET

To print all or a portion of your worksheet, use the following directions, which are given for the Epson printer (compressed font).

Place your cursor on A1 and type:

/P	starts PRINT command
P	displays options
O	selects Options option
S	Selects Setup option and displays: Enter Setup String
\015	sets an Epson printer to compressed font
RETURN	accepts setup and displays options
M	selects Margin option
R	selects Right option
230	characters per line
RETURN	displays options
Q	selects Quit option and returns to main print menu
R	displays Range to print from
.	ellipsis - indicates from-to

Move cursor, with arrow keys, to last coordinate in area you wish to print. The screen will reverse to indicate the area being printed.

RETURN	executes the command

G   selects Go option and prints

To exit out of PRINT command, type:

Q   selects Quit option and exits out of PRINT command

LOADING YOUR WORKSHEET BACK INTO LOTUS 1-2-3

At a later date, when you need to use the worksheet to do further computations, just load your worksheet back into memory.

To do this, you must first clear memory if there is anything in it. To clear the memory,

Leave your cursor on any location and type:

/W   starts WORKSHEET command

E   selects Erase option

Y   Yes, to confirm

Now you are ready to load the worksheet into the memory, using 1-2-3's FILE command. To do this,

Place the data diskette from which you wish to load into Drive A.

Leave your cursor on any location and type:

/F   starts FILE command

R   selects Retrieve option

Place your cursor on the file name you wish to load, and press:

RETURN   executes the command

CHAPTER SEVENTEEN

ECONOMIC ORDER QUANTITY

DESCRIPTION

Economic order quantity means the quantity which needs to be ordered in order to minimize inventory costs during a specified time period, assuming no stockouts. When determining inventory costs, one must consider the ordering costs plus carrying costs. In this exercise, we will determine the economic order quantity and the minimum inventory costs for the time period, as well as the number of times it will be necessary to order.

EXAMPLE

One of the aims of the Woodstock Manufacturing Company is to keep their inventory costs down. They need to order 30,000 units each year. Each purchase order placed costs $18. They have estimated that it costs them $.15 to carry one unit for a year.

The company wants to know what their economic order quantity (EOQ) is, and also what the minimum yearly inventory costs are. They are assuming that their carrying costs will rise to $.25 per unit, and they need to know how the EOQ and their inventory costs will be affected. They also want to know how often it will be necessary to order.

SETTING UP YOUR WORKSHEET - ENTERING LABELS

USE THE FOLLOWING STEP-BY-STEP DIRECTIONS FOR ENTERING THE LABELS IN FIGURE 1:

Enter your labels, starting in A1 and continuing through A13, exactly as illustrated in Figure 1, retaining exact row and column locations of all information.

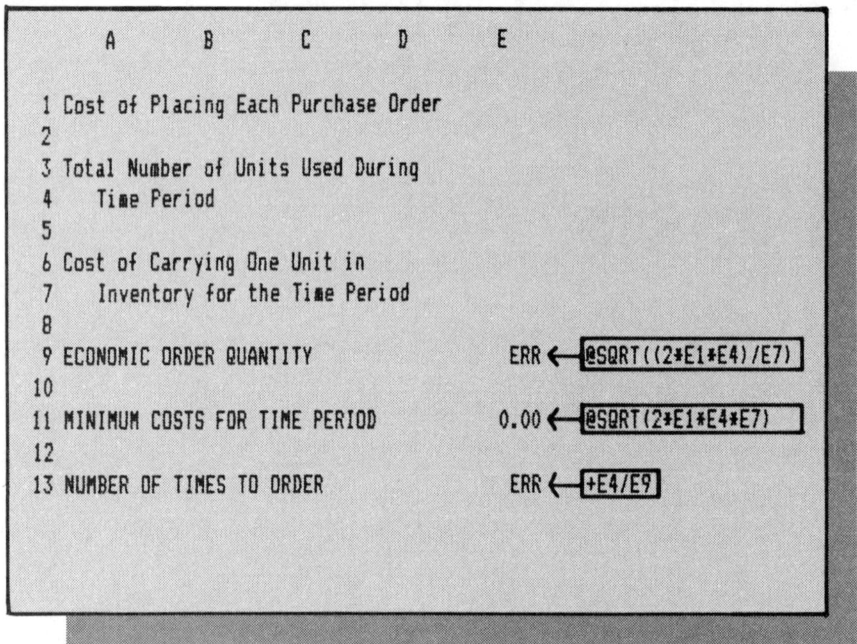

Figure 1

Now that you have entered your labels, you will begin entering the formulas which will calculate the unknown values.

ENTERING FORMULAS

USE THE FOLLOWING STEP-BY-STEP DIRECTIONS FOR ENTERING THE FORMULAS WHICH WILL CALCULATE THE UNKNOWN VALUES.

Formula one in column E, to the right of ECONOMIC ORDER QUANTITY, computes the economic order quantity.

Place your cursor on E9 and type:

@SQRT ((2 * E1 * E4) / E7)   formula

RETURN   enters the formula

Formula two is in column E, to the right of MINIMUM COSTS FOR TIME PERIOD.

Place your cursor on E11 and type:

@SQRT (2 * E1 * E4 * E7)	formula
RETURN	enters the formula

Formula three, in column E, to the right of NUMBER OF TIMES TO ORDER, calculates the number of times it will be necessary to order.

Place your cursor on E13 and type:

+ E4 / E9	formula
RETURN	enters the formula

Now you will format the coordinates into which you have entered formulas one and two, so that they will be displayed with two decimal places. To do this,

Place your cursor on E9 and type:

/R	starts RANGE command
F	selects Format option
F	selects Fixed option and displays number of decimal places: 2
RETURN	displays Range to format: E9

Move your cursor, with the arrow keys, to E11. The screen will reverse to show which coordinates are being formatted.

RETURN	executes the command

Last, you will want to format the coordinate into which you entered formula three, so that it will be displayed as an integer.

Place your cursor on E13 and type:

/R	starts RANGE command
F	selects Format option
F	selects Fixed option and displays number of decimal places:
0	number of decimal places
RETURN	displays range to format: E13
RETURN	executes the command

Your worksheet should now look like Figure 1.

MAKING WORKSHEET ENTRIES

___________________ NOTE ___________________

Never enter values into coordinates containing formulas, or the formulas will be erased.

Now that you have entered all the formulas, make your worksheet entries, into Column E, in rows 1, 4 and 7, as illustrated in Figure 2.

```
       A          B         C         D         E

 1 Cost of Placing Each Purchase Order        18
 2
 3 Total Number of Units Used During
 4    Time Period                          30000
 5
 6 Cost of Carrying One Unit in
 7    Inventory for the Time Period         0.15
 8
 9 ECONOMIC ORDER QUANTITY                 2683.28
10
11 MINIMUM COSTS FOR TIME PERIOD            402.49
12
13 NUMBER OF TIMES TO ORDER                    11
```

Figure 2

Now that your worksheet is complete, it is ready and all you need to do is enter your own set of known values.

SAVING YOUR WORKSHEET

Now save your worksheet for future use, so that the next time you wish to figure these computations all you will need to do is enter in your new known values, and you will not need to retype in the labels or enter the formulas.

To save your worksheet, place a formatted data diskette in Drive A.

With your cursor on any location, type:

/F	starts FILE command
S	selects Save option

Type in name of file.

RETURN	executes the command

PRINTING YOUR WORKSHEET

To print all or a portion of your worksheet, use the following directions, which are given for the Epson printer (compressed font).

Place your cursor on A1 and type:

/P	starts PRINT command
P	displays options
O	selects Options option
S	Selects Setup option and displays: Enter Setup String
\015	sets an Epson printer to compressed font
RETURN	accepts setup and displays options
M	selects Margin option
R	selects Right option
230	characters per line
RETURN	displays options
Q	selects Quit option and returns to main print menu
R	displays Range to print from
.	ellipsis - indicates from-to

Move cursor, with arrow keys, to last coordinate in area you wish to print. The screen will reverse to indicate the area being printed.

RETURN	executes the command
G	selects Go option and prints

To exit out of PRINT command, type:

Q	selects Quit option and exits out of PRINT command

LOADING YOUR WORKSHEET BACK INTO LOTUS 1-2-3

At a later date, when you need to use the worksheet to do further computations, just load your worksheet back into memory.

To do this, you must first clear memory if there is anything in it. To clear the memory,

Leave your cursor on any location and type:

/W	starts WORKSHEET command
E	selects Erase option
Y	Yes, to confirm

Now you are ready to load the worksheet into the memory, using 1-2-3's FILE command. To do this,

Place the data diskette from which you wish to load into Drive A.

Leave your cursor on any location and type:

/F	starts FILE command
R	selects Retrieve option

Place your cursor on the file name you wish to load, and press:

RETURN	executes the command

CHAPTER EIGHTEEN

COST VOLUME PROFIT ANALYSIS

DESCRIPTION

In this exercise an analysis of cost-volume-profit includes the determination of the sales volumes (in dollars and cents) needed in order to earn a specified amount after taxes, the after-tax income that would be produced by a specified amount of sales, the breakeven point in sales dollars, and the breakeven point in units sold.

EXAMPLE

The advertising department of a shoe company is planning a sales campaign to promote its new jogging shoes, and wants to determine how much it can budget for the promotion.

Their shoes sell for $20 a pair. The unit variable cost is $15, and the fixed costs in dollars is $3,000. The tax rate percent of income before taxes is 40%. The desired after-tax income is $2500.

They want to determine the unit sales necessary to earn $2500 after taxes, and the after tax income for sales of 1700 units. They also want to know the dollars needed to earn after-tax income ($2500 net), and the after-tax income for sales volume of $34,000. Finally they want to determine the breakeven point in sales dollars, as well as the breakeven point in units.

SETTING UP YOUR WORKSHEET - ENTERING LABELS

USE THE FOLLOWING STEP-BY-STEP DIRECTIONS FOR ENTERING THE LABELS IN FIGURE 1:

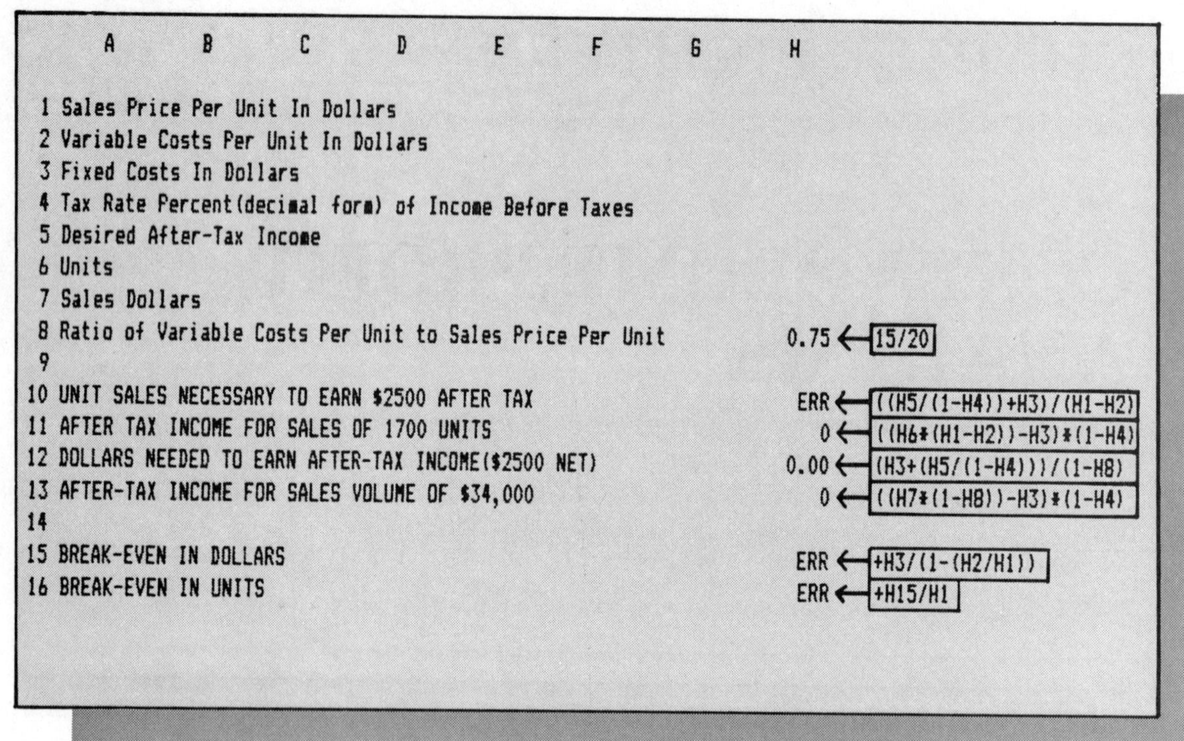

Figure 1

First, column H needs to be expanded to allow for 12 characters.

Place your cursor on column H and type:

/W	starts WORKSHEET command
C	selects Column-Width option
S	selects Set option
12	number of spaces in column
RETURN	executes the command

Now enter your labels, starting in A1 and continuing through A16, exactly as illustrated in Figure 1, retaining exact row and column locations of all information.

Now that you have entered your labels, you will begin entering the formulas which will calculate the unknown values.

ENTERING FORMULAS

USE THE FOLLOWING STEP-BY-STEP DIRECTIONS FOR ENTERING THE FORMULAS WHICH WILL CALCULATE THE UNKNOWN VALUES.

Formula one, in column H, is the Ratio of Variable Costs Per Unit to Sales Price Per Unit.

Place your cursor on H8 and type:

15/20	variable costs/sales price ratio
RETURN	enters the formula

Formula two, in column H, is the Unit Sales Necessary To Earn $2500 After Tax.

Place your cursor on H10 and type:

((H 5 / (1 — H 4)) + H 3) / (H 1 — H 2)	formula
RETURN	enters the formula

You now need to format the coordinate into which you have just entered the formula so that later it will be displayed with 2 decimal places.

Leave your cursor on H10 and type:

/R	starts RANGE command
F	selects Format option
F	selects Fixed option and displays number of decimal places: 2
RETURN	displays Range to format: H10
RETURN	executes the command

Formula three in column H is the After Tax Income For Sales Of 1700 Units.

Place your cursor on H11 and type:

((H 6 * (H 1 — H 2)) — H 3) * (1 — H 4)	formula
RETURN	enters the formula

Formula four in column H is the Dollars Needed To Earn After-Tax Income ($2500 net).

Place your cursor on H12 and type:

(H3 + (H5 / (1 — H4))) / (1 — H8)   formula

| RETURN | enters the formula

Now you will format the coordinate into which you have just entered the formula so that it will later be displayed with two decimal places.

Leave your cursor on H12 and type:

/R   starts RANGE command

F   selects Format option

F   selects Fixed option and displays number of decimal places: 2

| RETURN | displays Range to format: H12

| RETURN | executes the command

Formula five in column H, is the After-Tax Income For Sales Volume of $34,000.

Place your cursor on H13 and type:

((H7 * (1 — H8)) — H3) * (1 — H4)   formula

| RETURN | enters the formula

Formula six, in column H, is the Break-Even Amount in Dollars.

Place your cursor on H15 and type:

+ H3 / (1 — (H2 / H1))   formula

| RETURN | enters the formula

Now you will format the coordinates into which you have just entered the formula so that it will be displayed as currency, with two decimal places.

Leave your cursor on H15 and type:

/R   starts RANGE command

F   selects Format option

C   selects Currency option and displays # of decimal places: 2

RETURN   displays range to format: H15

RETURN   executes the command

Formula seven, in column H, is the Break-Even Amount in Units.

Place your cursor on H16 and type:

+ H 1 5 / H 1   formula

RETURN   enters the formula

Your worksheet should now look like Figure 1.

MAKING WORKSHEET ENTRIES

_____________ NOTE _____________

Never enter values into cells containing formulas, or the formulas will be erased.

Now that you have entered all the formulas, make your worksheet entries, in Column H, in Rows 1 through 7, as illustrated in Figure 2.

```
              A      B      C      D      E      F      G      H

 1 Sales Price Per Unit In Dollars                                      20
 2 Variable Costs Per Unit In Dollars                                   15
 3 Fixed Costs In Dollars                                             3000
 4 Tax Rate Percent(decimal form) of Income Before Taxes              0.4
 5 Desired After-Tax Income                                           2500
 6 Units                                                              1700
 7 Sales Dollars                                                     34000
 8 Ration of Variable Costs Per Unit to Sales Price Per Unit          0.75
 9
10 UNIT SALES NECESSARY TO EARN $2500 AFTER TAX                     1433.33
11 AFTER TAX INCOME FOR SALES OF 1700 UNITS                            3300
12 DOLLARS NEEDED TO EARN AFTER-TAX INCOME($2500 NET)              28666.67
13 AFTER-TAX INCOME FOR SALES VOLUME OF $34,000                       3300
14
15 BREAK-EVEN IN DOLLARS                                         $12,000.00
16 BREAK-EVEN IN UNITS                                                  600
```

Figure 2

Now that your worksheet is complete, it is ready and all you need to do is enter your own set of known values.

SAVING YOUR WORKSHEET

Now save your worksheet for future use, so that the next time you wish to figure these computation all you will need to do is enter in your new known values, and you will not need to retype in the labels or enter the formula.

To save your worksheet, place a formatted data diskette in Drive A.

With your cursor on any location, type:

/F   starts FILE command

S   selects Save option

Type in name of file.

RETURN   executes the command

PRINTING YOUR WORKSHEET

To print all or a portion of your worksheet, use the following directions, which are given for the Epson printer (compressed font).

Place your cursor on A1 and type:

/P	starts PRINT command
P	displays options
O	selects Options option
S	Selects Setup option and displays: Enter Setup String
\015	sets an Epson printer to compressed font
RETURN	accepts setup and displays options
M	selects Margin option
R	selects Right option
230	characters per line
RETURN	displays options
Q	selects Quit option and returns to main print menu
R	displays Range to print from
.	ellipsis - indicates from-to

Move cursor, with arrow keys, to last coordinate in area you wish to print. The screen will reverse to indicate the area being printed.

RETURN	executes the command
G	selects Go option and prints

To exit out of **PRINT** command, type:

Q	selects Quit option and exits out of PRINT command

LOADING YOUR WORKSHEET BACK INTO LOTUS 1-2-3

At a later date, when you need to use the worksheet to do further computations, just load your worksheet back into memory.

To do this, you must first clear memory if there is anything in it. To clear the memory,

Leave your cursor on any location and type:

/W   starts WORKSHEET command

E   selects Erase option

Y   Yes, to confirm

Now you are ready to load the worksheet into the memory, using 1-2-3's FILE command. To do this,

Place the data diskette from which you wish to load into Drive A.

Leave your cursor on any location and type:

/F   starts FILE command

R   selects Retrieve option

Place your cursor on the file name you wish to load, and press:

RETURN   executes the command

CHAPTER NINETEEN

FINDING THE MEAN, STANDARD DEVIATION AND VARIANCE OF A POPULATION

DESCRIPTION

When a set of data is set up for study, statistical calculations are used to explain and describe the data. One of the most common computations is determining the mean, or average, of the data given. Another useful calculation is finding the standard deviation, (commonly referred to as the spread or distribution of the data points). It is also useful to know the extent to which, or range in which, a thing varies, which is called the variance.

EXAMPLE

A word processing school gives periodic tests to its students in order to assess their advancement. The highest possible score in the test is 10. The test was given to 5 of the students.

The school now needs to know the mean, the standard deviation, and the variance.

SETTING UP YOUR WORKSHEET - ENTERING LABELS

USE THE FOLLOWING STEP-BY-STEP DIRECTIONS FOR ENTERING THE LABELS IN FIGURE 1:

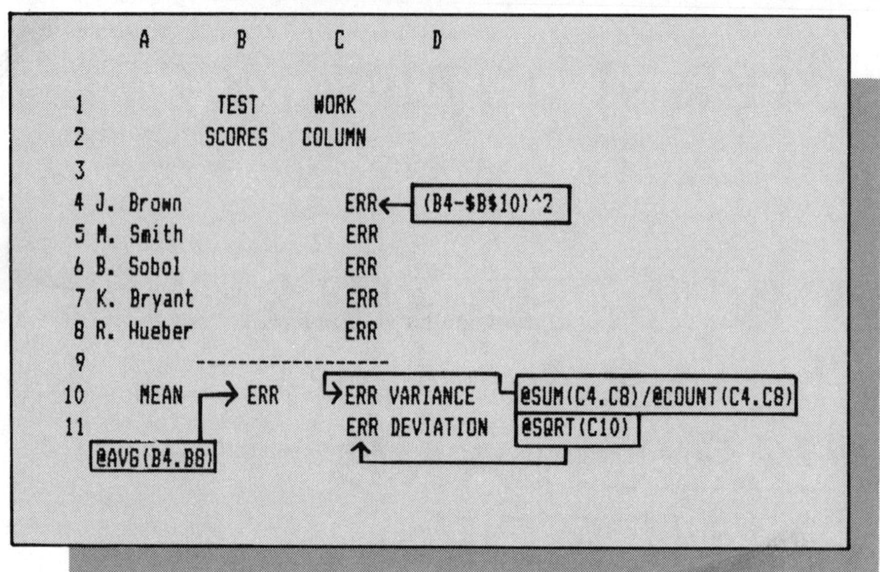

Figure 1

Begin entering your labels, starting with rows 1 and 2, in columns B and C. Then you will center the labels you have just entered. to do this,

Place your cursor on B1 and type:

/R	starts RANGE command
L	selects Label option
C	selects Center option and displays B1

Move your cursor, with arrow keys, to C2. The screen will reverse to show you the area being centered.

RETURN	executes the command

Next enter the labels representing the students' names. Begin in A4 and continue down through A8. Then enter the label, MEAN, in A10.

Now you will right-justify the labels you have just entered in column A.

Place your cursor on A4 and type:

/R	starts RANGE command
L	selects Label option
R	selects Right option and displays A4

Move your cursor, with arrow keys, to A10. Screen will reverse to show you the area being right-justified.

RETURN	executes the command

Now enter the label, VARIANCE, in D10. Then enter the label DEVIATION in D11.

Last enter the dashed lines in row 9. To do this,

Place your cursor on B9 and type:

\	starts REPEAT command
—	label to be repeated

RETURN	executes the command

To copy the dashed line across into column C,

Leave your cursor on B9 and type:

/C	starts COPY command and displays B9

RETURN	displays range to copy to
C9	range to copy to

RETURN	executes the command

Now that you have entered your labels and the dashed line, you will begin entering the formulas which will calculate the unknown values.

ENTERING FORMULAS

USE THE FOLLOWING STEP-BY-STEP DIRECTIONS FOR ENTERING THE FORMULAS WHICH WILL CALCULATE THE UNKNOWN VALUES.

Formula one, in column B, to the right of MEAN, immediately underneath the dashed line, will calculate the mean.

Place your cursor on B10 and type:

@AVG(B4.B8)   formula

RETURN   enters the formula

Formula two, in column C, at the top of WORK COLUMN, will generate the variance.

___ **NOTE** ___

1-2-3 is designed to do one of two things with coordinates when they are copied. The coordinates are either relative to their new location or they remain absolute, which means they remain the same.

A coordinate address is relative unless it is converted to an absolute by having a dollar sign ($) preceding the column designation and/or row designation, i.e. B10.

A quick way to make a coordinate absolute is by placing your cursor on that coordinate and pressing the F4 key, which will automatically place the dollar as shown.

In formula two, which you are about to enter, the value in B10 must remain absolute, when you copy the formula down the column later. You will note that, in order to accomplish this, when you enter the formula you will be typing B10.

To enter formula two,

Place your cursor on C4 and type:

(B4 — B10)^2   formula

RETURN   enters the formula

Now you will copy the formula you have just entered down the column to the dashed line. To do this,

Leave your cursor on C4 and type:

/C	starts COPY command and displays range to copy from: C4
RETURN	displays range to copy to
C5	first coordinate to copy to
.	ellipsis - indicating from-to
C8	last coordinate to copy to
RETURN	executes the command

Formula three, in column C, to the left of VARIANCE, immediately underneath the dashed line, calculates the variance from the work column.

Place your cursor on C10 and type:

@SUM (C 4 . C 8) / @COUNT (C 4 . C 8) formula	
RETURN	enters the formula

Formula four, in column C, to the left of DEVIATION, calculates the standard deviation.

Place your cursor on C11 and type:

@SQRT (C 1 0)	formula
RETURN	enters the formula

Your worksheet should now look like Figure 1.

MAKING WORKSHEET ENTRIES

NOTE

Never enter values into coordinates containing formulas, or the formulas will be erased.

Now that you have entered all the formulas, make your worksheet entries, typing in the test scores for the students, in column B, starting in B4, until you reach the dashed line, as illustrated in Figure 2.

```
              A        B        C        D

     1                TEST     WORK
     2               SCORES   COLUMN
     3
     4 J. Brown       4        4
     5 M. Smith       5        1
     6 B. Sobol       6        0
     7 K. Bryant      7        1
     8 R. Hueber      8        4
     9               -------------------
    10    MEAN        6            2 VARIANCE
    11                     1.414213 DEVIATION
```

Figure 2

Now that your worksheet is complete, it is ready and all you need to do is enter your own set of known values.

SAVING YOUR WORKSHEET

Now save your worksheet for future use, so that the next time you wish to figure these computations all you will need to do is enter in your new known values, and you will not need to retype in the labels or enter the formulas.

To save your worksheet, place a formatted data diskette in Drive A.

With your cursor on any location, type:

/F   starts FILE command

S   selects Save option

Type in name of file.

RETURN   executes the command

PRINTING YOUR WORKSHEET

To print all or a portion of your worksheet, use the following directions, which are given for the Epson printer (compressed font).

Place your cursor on A1 and type:

/P	starts PRINT command
P	displays options
O	selects Options option
S	Selects Setup option and displays: Enter Setup String
\015	sets an Epson printer to compressed font
RETURN	accepts setup and displays options
M	selects Margin option
R	selects Right option
230	characters per line
RETURN	displays options
Q	selects Quit option and returns to main print menu
R	displays Range to print from
.	ellipsis - indicates from-to

Move cursor, with arrow keys, to last coordinate in area you wish to print. The screen will reverse to indicate the area being printed.

RETURN	executes the command
G	selects Go option and prints

To exit out of PRINT command, type:

Q	selects Quit option and exits out of PRINT command

LOADING YOUR WORKSHEET BACK INTO LOTUS 1-2-3

At a later date, when you need to use the worksheet to do further computations, just load your worksheet back into memory.

To do this, you must first clear memory if there is anything in it. To clear the memory,

Leave your cursor on any location and type:

/W   starts WORKSHEET command

E   selects Erase option

Y   Yes, to confirm

Now you are ready to load the worksheet into the memory, using 1-2-3's FILE command. To do this,

Place the data diskette from which you wish to load into Drive A.

Leave your cursor on any location and type:

/F   starts FILE command

R   selects Retrieve option

Place your cursor on the file name you wish to load, and press:

| RETURN | executes the command

CHAPTER TWENTY

FINDING THE MEAN, STANDARD DEVIATION AND STANDARD ERROR OF MEAN FOR A SAMPLE

DESCRIPTION

When a set of statistics which has been derived from a sampling is being studied, certain calculations have to be performed in order to fully evaluate the meaning of the statistics. It is advisable to calculate the mean, the standard error of that mean, as well as the standard deviation, of the statistics being analyzed.

EXAMPLE

A retail chain store has two top salespersons. The manager wants to compare the daily sales of its two star salespersons for a 20-day period.

He wants to know what the average daily sales of each salesperson are, and the standard deviation of each salesperson's sales, as well as the standard error of mean.

SETTING UP YOUR WORKSHEET - ENTERING LABELS

USE THE FOLLOWING STEP-BY-STEP DIRECTIONS FOR ENTERING THE LABELS IN FIGURE 1:

First enter the labels in rows 1 and 2, in columns A, C, E and G, exactly as illustrated in Figure 1, retaining exact row and column locations of all information.

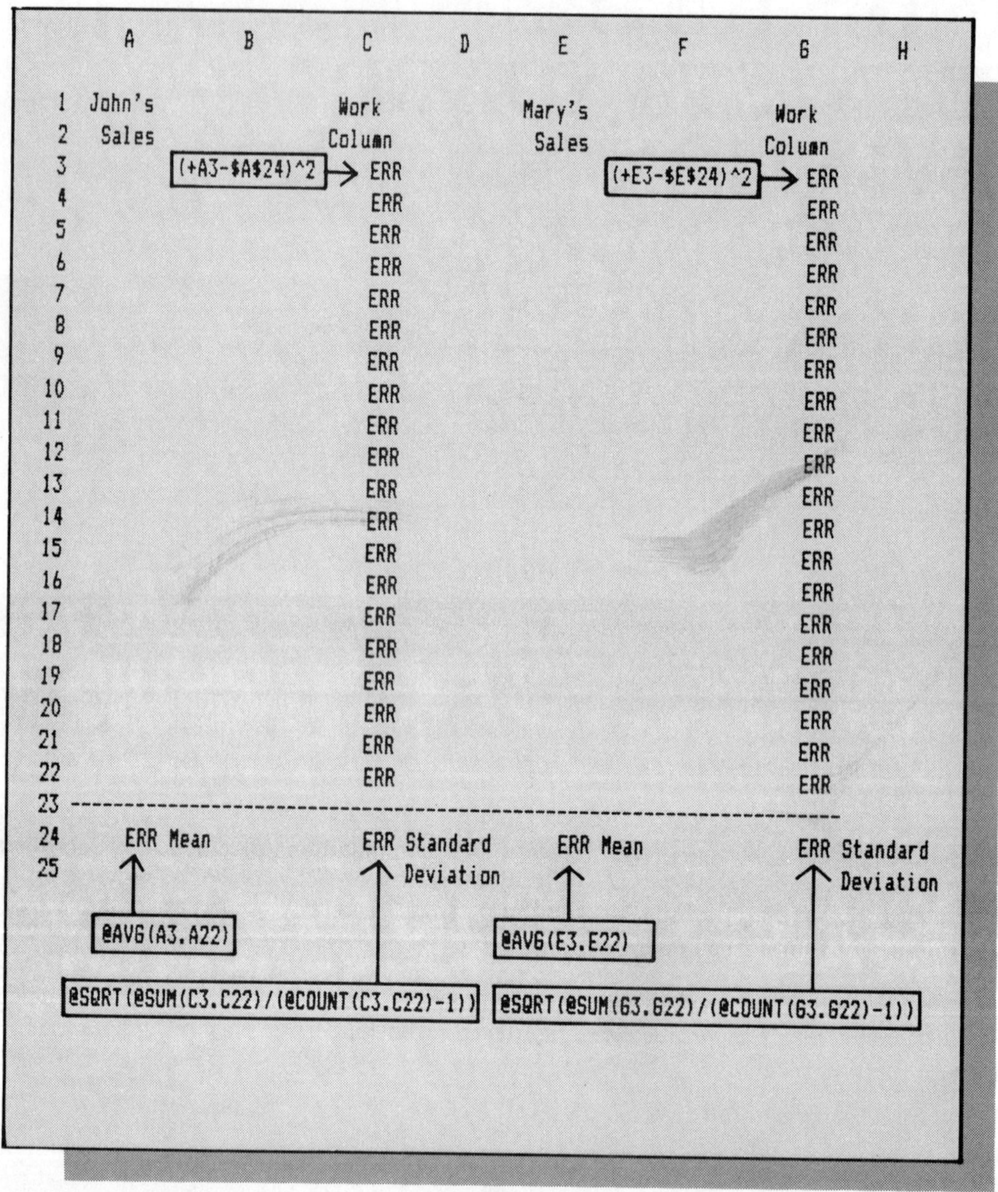

Figure 1

Next you will center the labels you have just entered in rows 1 and 2. To do this,

Place your cursor on A1 and type:

/R	starts RANGE command
L	selects Label option
C	selects Center option and displays A1

Move your cursor, with arrow keys, to G2. The screen will reverse to show which coordinates are being centered.

RETURN	executes the command

Now enter the labels in row 24, as follows:

Enter Mean in column B.
Enter Standard in column D.
Enter Mean in column F.
Enter Standard in column H.

Last enter the labels in row 25.

Enter Deviation in column D.
Enter Deviation in column H.

Now enter the dashed line in row 23.

Place your cursor on A23 and type:

\	starts REPEAT command
—	label to be repeated
RETURN	executes the command

Next, copy the dashed line across row 23.

Leave your cursor on A23 and type:

/C	starts COPY command and displays A23, coordinate to copy from
RETURN	displays range to copy to
B23	first coordinate to copy to
.	ellipsis - indicates from-to
G23	last coordinate to copy to
RETURN	executes the command

Now that you have entered your labels and the dashed line, you will begin entering the formulas which will calculate the unknown values.

ENTERING FORMULAS

USE THE FOLLOWING STEP-BY-STEP DIRECTIONS FOR ENTERING THE FORMULAS WHICH WILL CALCULATE THE UNKNOWN VALUES.

Formula one, in column A, to the left of MEAN, immediately underneath the dashed line, calculates John's Mean.

Place your cursor on A24 and type:

@AVG(A3.A22)   formula

RETURN   enters the formula

Formula two, in column E, to the left of MEAN, immediately underneath the dashed line, calculates Mary's Mean.

Place your cursor on E24 and type:

@AVG(E3.E22)   formula

RETURN   enters the formula

Formula three in column C, immediately underneath Work Column, calculates John's standard deviation, for his first day's sales.

NOTE

1-2-3 is designed to do one of two things with coordinates when they are copied. The coordinates are either relative to their new location or they remain absolute, which means they remain the same.

A coordinate address is relative unless it is converted to an absolute by having a dollar sign ($) preceding the column designation and/or row designation, i.e. A24.

A quick way to make a coordinate absolute is by placing your cursor on that coordinate and pressing the F4 key, which will automatically place the dollar as shown.

In formula three, which you are about to enter, the value in A24 must remain absolute, when you copy the formula down the column later. You will note that, in order to accomplish this, when you enter the formula you will be typing A24.

To enter formula three, place your cursor on C3 and type:

(+ A 3 — $ A $ 2 4)^2   formula

RETURN   enters the formula

Now you will copy this formula down the Work Column, to the dashed line.

Leave your cursor on C3 and type:

/C	starts COPY command and displays C3, coordinate to be copied
RETURN	displays Range to copy to
C4	first coordinate to copy to
.	ellipsis - indicates from-to
C22	last coordinate to copy to
RETURN	executes the command

Formula four in column G, immediately underneath Work Column, calculates Mary's standard deviation, for her first day's sales.

Place your cursor on G3 and type:

$(+ E\,3 - \$\,E\,\$\,2\,4\,)\,\hat{}\,2$	formula
RETURN	enters the formula

Now you will format the coordinate into which you have entered the formula so that it will be displayed with two decimal places.

Leave your cursor on G3 and type:

/R	starts RANGE command
F	selects Format option
F	selects Fixed option and displays number of decimal places: 2
RETURN	displays Range to format: G3
RETURN	executes the command

Now you will copy this formula down the Work Column, to the dashed line.

Leave your cursor on G3 and type:

/C	starts COPY command and displays G3, coordinate to copy from
RETURN	displays Range to copy to
G4	first coordinate to copy to
.	ellipsis - indicates from-to
G22	last coordinate to copy to
RETURN	executes the command

Formula five in column C, to the left of Standard Deviation, immediately underneath the dashed line, calculates the standard deviation for all of John's sales.

Place your cursor on C24 and type:

@SQRT (@SUM (C 3 . C 2 2) / (@COUNT (C 3 . C 2 2) — 1))   formula

RETURN   enters the formula

Formula six, in column G, to the left of Standard Deviation, immediately underneath the dashed line, calculates the standard deviation for all of Mary's sales.

Place your cursor on G24 and type:

@SQRT (@SUM (G 3 , G 2 2) / (@COUNT (G 3 . G 2 2) — 1))   formula

RETURN   enters the formula

Now you will format some of the coordinates into which you have entered formulas so that later they will be displayed with two decimal places.

Place your cursor on C24 and type:

/R   starts RANGE command

F   selects Format option

F   selects Fixed option and displays number of decimal places: 2

RETURN   displays Range to format: C24

Move your cursor to G24. Screen will reverse to show which coordinates are being formatted.

RETURN   executes the command

Your worksheet should now look like Figure 1.

MAKING WORKSHEET ENTRIES

NOTE

Never enter values into coordinates containing formulas, or the formulas will be erased.

Now that you have entered all the formulas, make your worksheet entries, as illustrated in Figure 2. To do this,

	A	B	C	D	E	F	G	H
1	John's		Work		Mary's		Work	
2	Sales		Column		Sales		Column	
3	650		870.25		600		588.06	
4	625		20.25		660		1278.06	
5	600		420.25		700		5738.06	
6	675		2970.25		670		2093.06	
7	650		870.25		620		18.06	
8	625		20.25		580		1958.06	
9	610		110.25		630		33.06	
10	590		930.25		570		2943.06	
11	580		1640.25		600		588.06	
12	595		650.25		690		4323.06	
13	630		90.25		640		248.06	
14	610		110.25		560		4128.06	
15	640		380.25		500		15438.06	
16	620		0.25		575		2425.56	
17	635		210.25		640		248.06	
18	620		0.25		650		663.06	
19	615		30.25		680		3108.06	
20	605		240.25		720		9168.06	
21	625		20.25		620		18.06	
22	610		110.25		580		1958.06	
23	---							
24	620.5 Mean		22.59 Standard		624.25 Mean		54.75 Standard	
25			Deviation				Deviation	

Figure 2

Place your cursor on A3 and type:

650	John's sales for the first day

RETURN	enters the value

Continue typing in John's sales down the column, until you reach the dashed line.

Then place your cursor on E3 and type:

600	Mary's sales for the first day

RETURN	enters the value

Continue typing in Mary's sales down the column, until you reach the dashed line.

Now that your worksheet is complete, it is ready and all you need to do is enter your own set of known values.

SAVING YOUR WORKSHEET

Now save your worksheet for future use, so that the next time you wish to figure these computations all you will need to do is enter in your new known values, and you will not need to retype in the labels or enter the formulas.

To save your worksheet, place a formatted data diskette in Drive A.

With your cursor on any location, type:

/F	starts FILE command
S	selects Save option

Type in name of file.

RETURN	executes the command

PRINTING YOUR WORKSHEET

To print all or a portion of your worksheet, use the following directions, which are given for the Epson printer (compressed font).

Place your cursor on A1 and type:

/P	starts PRINT command
P	displays options
O	selects Options option
S	Selects Setup option and displays: Enter Setup String

\015	sets an Epson printer to compressed font
RETURN	accepts setup and displays options
M	selects Margin option
R	selects Right option
230	characters per line
RETURN	displays options
Q	selects Quit option and returns to main print menu
R	displays Range to print from
.	ellipsis - indicates from-to

Move cursor, with arrow keys, to last coordinate in area you wish to print. The screen will reverse to indicate the area being printed.

RETURN	executes the command
G	selects Go option and prints

To exit out of PRINT command, type:

Q	selects Quit option and exits out of PRINT command

LOADING YOUR WORKSHEET BACK INTO LOTUS 1-2-3

At a later date, when you need to use the worksheet to do further computations, just load your worksheet back into memory.

To do this, you must first clear memory if there is anything in it. To clear the memory,

Leave your cursor on any location and type:

/W	starts WORKSHEET command
E	selects Erase option
Y	Yes, to confirm

Now you are ready to load the worksheet into the memory, using 1-2-3's FILE command. To do this,

Place the data diskette from which you wish to load into Drive A.

Leave your cursor on any location and type:

/F	starts FILE command
R	selects Retrieve option

Place your cursor on the file name you wish to load, and press:

RETURN	executes the command

CHAPTER TWENTY-ONE

CONSIDERING A HUGE POPULATION WITH A LARGE SAMPLING

DESCRIPTION

When considering a large sampling which has been taken from a huge population, you must first decide on the degree of certainty you wish to obtain when calculating the range in which the population mean will lie. It is also necessary to restore the randomness of your population, because when you test the items in a sampling you remove them from the population and they cannot be returned after testing.

Then, based on the population size, the size of the sampling, the mean lifetime of the sample, the standard deviation of the population and the degree of certainty you desire, you can calculate the upper and lower limit for the actual population mean.

EXAMPLE

The Nantucket Manufacturing Company regularly tests the light bulbs which it manufactures. In their latest test, the company took a sampling of 100 light bulbs out of its last batch of 5000. The degree of certainty they seek is 95%. The sample mean lifetime is 175 hours, and the standard deviation of the population is 18 hours.

The company wants to determine the upper and lower limits for the actual population mean. They also need to know the actual quantity, with the randomness restored after removal of the sample items.

SETTING UP YOUR WORKSHEET - ENTERING LABELS

USE THE FOLLOWING STEP-BY-STEP DIRECTIONS FOR ENTERING THE LABELS IN FIGURE 1:

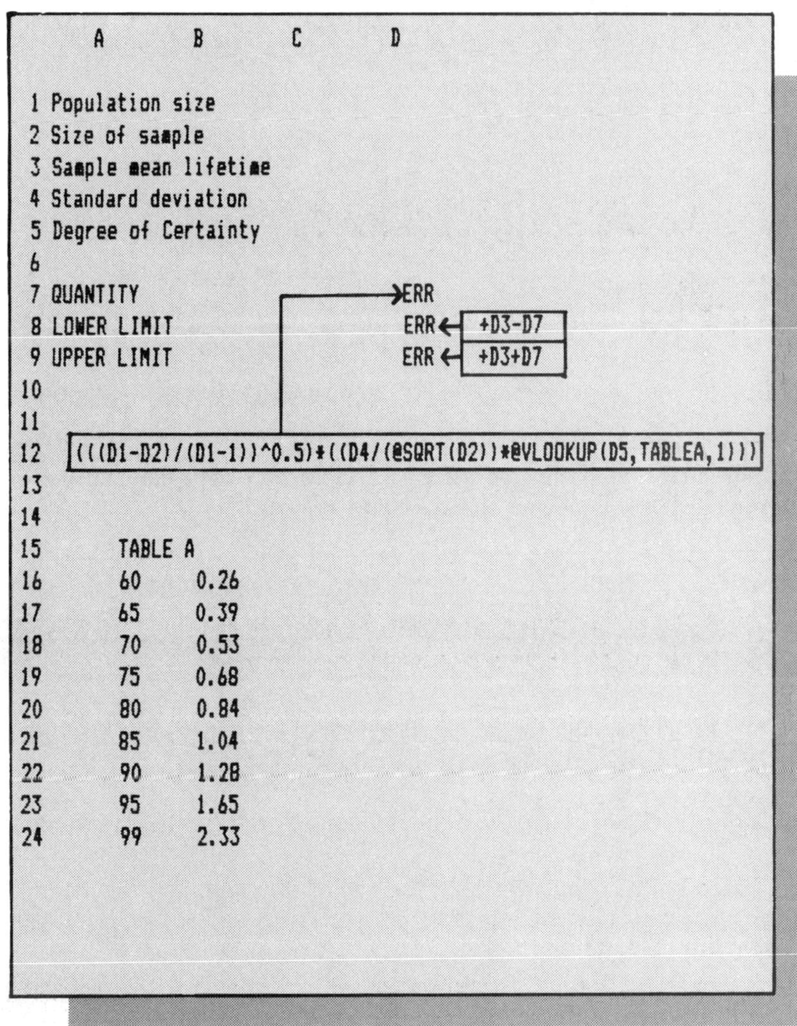

Figure 1

Enter your labels, starting in A1, and continue through A9, exactly as illustrated in Figure 1, retaining exact row and column locations of all information.

Next type in TABLE A at the bottom of your worksheet, retaining exact row and column locations of all information.

NAMING TABLE A

Now that you have entered your labels and typed in TABLE A at the bottom of your worksheet, you will name TABLE A, because you will be using it later in a formula. To name TABLE A,

Place your cursor on A16 and type:

/R	starts RANGE command
N	selects Name option
C	selects Create option
TABLEA	name given to table
RETURN	displays Range A16, upper left-hand corner of table to be named

Move your cursor, with the arrow keys, to B24, lower right-hand corner of table to be named. The screen will reverse to show you the area being named.

RETURN	executes the command

ENTERING FORMULAS

USE THE FOLLOWING STEP-BY-STEP DIRECTIONS FOR ENTERING THE FORMULAS WHICH WILL CALCULATE THE UNKNOWN VALUES.

Formula one, in column D, to the right of Quantity, restores the randomness of your selection.

> **NOTE**
>
> In formula one, which you are about to enter, the LOOKUP function will be used to look up a value TABLE A.
>
> The table in this exercise is in a column format, which means that it is in a Vertical format. Therefore, the LOOKUP function being used will be indicated by @VLOOKUP. (The V indicates that the table is in Vertical, or column, format.)
>
> The left-most column of the table is considered the labels of the table, and the adjacent column to the right contains the values. This adjacent column to the right is called the first offset. In formula one, which you are about toenter, the 1 after TableA refers to this first offset.
>
> If the table were in a row format, or a Horizontal format, the LOOKUP function being used would be indicated by @HLOOKUP, the H indicating that the table is in Horizontal, or row format. Then the top-most row would be considered the labels of the table, and the row beneath it would contain the values, and would be called the first offset.

Place your cursor on D7 and type:

$(((D1 - D2) / (D1 - 1))\,\hat{}\,0.5) * ((D4 / (@SQRT (D2)) * @VLOOKUP (D5, TABLEA , 1)))$ formula

RETURN   enters the formula

Formula two, in column D, to the right of Lower Limit, calculates the lower limit for the actual population mean.

Place your cursor on D8 and type:

+ D 3 — D 7   formula

RETURN   enters the formula

Formula three, in column D, to the right of Upper Limit, calculates the upper limit for the actual population mean.

Place your cursor on D9 and type:

+ D 3 + D 7   formula

RETURN   enters the formula

Now you will format the coordinates into which you have just entered the formulas, so that they will be displayed with two decimals.

Place your cursor on D7 and type:

/R	starts RANGE command
F	selects Format option
F	selects Fixed option and displays number of decimal places: 2
RETURN	displays Range to format: D7

Move your cursor, with arrow keys, to D9. The screen will reverse to show you the area being formatted.

RETURN	executes the command

Your worksheet should now look like Figure 1.

MAKING WORKSHEET ENTRIES

NOTE

Never enter values into coordinates containing formulas, or the formulas will be erased.

Now that you have entered all the formulas, make your worksheet entries, beginning in D1, and continuing through D5, as illustrated in Figure 2.

	A	B	C	D
1	Population size			5000
2	Size of sample			100
3	Sample mean lifetime			175
4	Standard deviation			18
5	Degree of Certainty			95
6				
7	QUANTITY			2.94
8	LOWER LIMIT			172.06
9	UPPER LIMIT			177.94
10				
11				
12				
13				
14				
15	TABLE A			
16	60	0.26		
17	65	0.39		
18	70	0.53		
19	75	0.68		
20	80	0.84		
21	85	1.04		
22	90	1.28		
23	95	1.65		
24	99	2.33		

Figure 2

Now that your worksheet is complete, it is ready and all you need to do is enter your own set of known values.

SAVING YOUR WORKSHEET

Now save your worksheet for future use, so that the next time you wish to figure these computations all you will need to do is enter in your new known values, and you will not need to retype in the labels or enter the formulas.

To save your worksheet, place a formatted data diskette in Drive A.

With your cursor on any location, type:

/F	starts FILE command
S	selects Save option

Type in name of file.

RETURN	executes the command

PRINTING YOUR WORKSHEET

To print all or a portion of your worksheet, use the following directions, which are given for the Epson printer (compressed font).

Place your cursor on A1 and type:

/P	starts PRINT command
P	displays options
O	selects Options option
S	Selects Setup option and displays: Enter Setup String
\015	sets an Epson printer to compressed font
RETURN	accepts setup and displays options
M	selects Margin option
R	selects Right option
230	characters per line
RETURN	displays options

Q	selects Quit option and returns to main print menu
R	displays Range to print from
.	ellipsis - indicates from-to

Move cursor, with arrow keys, to last coordinate in area you wish to print. The screen will reverse to indicate the area being printed.

| RETURN | executes the command |
| G | selects Go option and prints |

To exit out of PRINT command, type:

| Q | selects Quit option and exits out of PRINT command |

LOADING YOUR WORKSHEET BACK INTO LOTUS 1-2-3

At a later date, when you need to use the worksheet to do further computations, just load your worksheet back into memory.

To do this, you must first clear memory if there is anything in it. To clear the memory,

Leave your cursor on any location and type:

/W	starts WORKSHEET command
E	selects Erase option
Y	Yes, to confirm

Now you are ready to load the worksheet into the memory, using 1-2-3's FILE command. To do this,

Place the data diskette from which you wish to load into Drive A.

Leave your cursor on any location and type:

| /F | starts FILE command |
| R | selects Retrieve option |

Place your cursor on the file name you wish to load, and press:

| RETURN | executes the command |

CHAPTER TWENTY-TWO

CONSIDER A HUGE POPULATION WITH A SMALL SAMPLING

DESCRIPTION

When the number of items in a sampling is under 30, it is referred to as a 'small' sampling. When it is preferable to take a small sampling, because of the sometimes high cost of the sampling procedure, there is a special statistical method designed especially for this situation.

The method allows for the calculation of a predicted range of values into which the population mean will fall, with the desired degree of certainty you have selected. The basis for any decision-making can be formed upon this predicted range of values.

EXAMPLE

A fruit juice processor, who bottles juice in five-gallon containers for restaurants, has been included in a government test to determine the amount of additives in each bottle. It is necessary that only a small sampling be used for gathering the statistics needed. A degree of certainty factor of 90% will be used.

The government wants to determine a predicted range of values into which the population mean will fall, as well as the upper and lower limits of the sampling.

> ______ **NOTE** ______
>
> Follow the step-by-step instructions EXACTLY. Although they are not in the usual sequence, the procedures themselves remain the same.
>
> The change in the sequence is deliberate and was planned in order to build the worksheet in the most efficient way possible.

SETTING UP YOUR WORKSHEET - ENTERING LABELS IN THE UPPER HALF OF YOUR WORKSHEET

USE THE FOLLOWING STEP-BY-STEP DIRECTIONS FOR ENTERING THE LABELS IN THE UPPER HALF OF FIGURE 1:

First, column A must be expanded to allow for long labels. To do this,

Place your cursor on column A and type:

/W	starts WORKSHEET command
C	selects Column-Width option
S	selects Set option
17	number of spaces in column
RETURN	executes the command

Now type in the labels in row 1 of your worksheet. Next you will center the labels in row 1.

Place your cursor on B1 and type:

/R	starts RANGE command
L	selects Label option
C	selects Center option and displays B1

Move your cursor, with the arrow keys, to C1. The screen will reverse to show you which coordinates are being centered.

RETURN	executes the command

SAMPLES WORK
First sample ERR ← (B2-B11)^2
Second sample ERR
Third sample ERR
Fourth sample ERR
Fifth sample ERR
Sixth sample ERR
Seventh sample ERR
Eighth sample ERR
@AVG(B2.B9)
Mean → ERR ERR ← Standard Deviation
(@SQRT(@SUM(C2.C9)/(@COUNT(C2.C9)-1)))
Deg. of Certainty 90
Deg. of Freedom 7 ← (@COUNT(C2.C9)-1)
From Table 1.895 ← @IF(B13=80,B20,@IF(B13=90,D20,@IF(B13=95,F20,@IF(B13=99,H20,J20))))
Upper Limit ERR ← +B11+((C11/@SQRT(@COUNT(C2.C9)))*B15)
Lower Limit ERR ← +B11-((C11/@SQRT(@COUNT(C2.C9)))*B15)
t1 t2 t3 t4 t5
Table80 → 1.415 Table90 → 1.895 Table95 → 2.365 Table99 → 3.499 Table99.9 5.405 ←
1 3.078 1 6.314 1 12.706 1 63.657 1 636.619
2 1.886 2 2.92 2 4.303 2 9.925 2 31.598
3 1.638 3 2.353 3 3.182 3 5.841 3 12.941
4 1.533 4 2.132 4 2.776 4 4.604 4 8.61
5 1.476 5 2.015 5 2.571 5 4.032 5 6.859
6 1.44 6 1.943 6 2.447 6 3.707 6 5.959
7 1.415 7 1.895 7 2.365 7 3.499 7 5.405
8 1.397 8 1.86 8 2.306 8 3.355 8 5.041
9 1.383 9 1.833 9 2.262 9 3.25 9 4.781
10 1.372 10 1.812 10 2.228 10 3.169 10 4.487
11 1.363 11 1.796 11 2.201 11 3.106 11 4.437
12 1.356 12 1.782 12 2.179 12 3.055 12 4.318
(@VLOOKUP(B14,Table80,1))
(@VLOOKUP(B14,Table90,1))
(@VLOOKUP(B14,Table95,1))
(@VLOOKUP(B14,Table99,1))
(@VLOOKUP(B14,Table99.9,1))

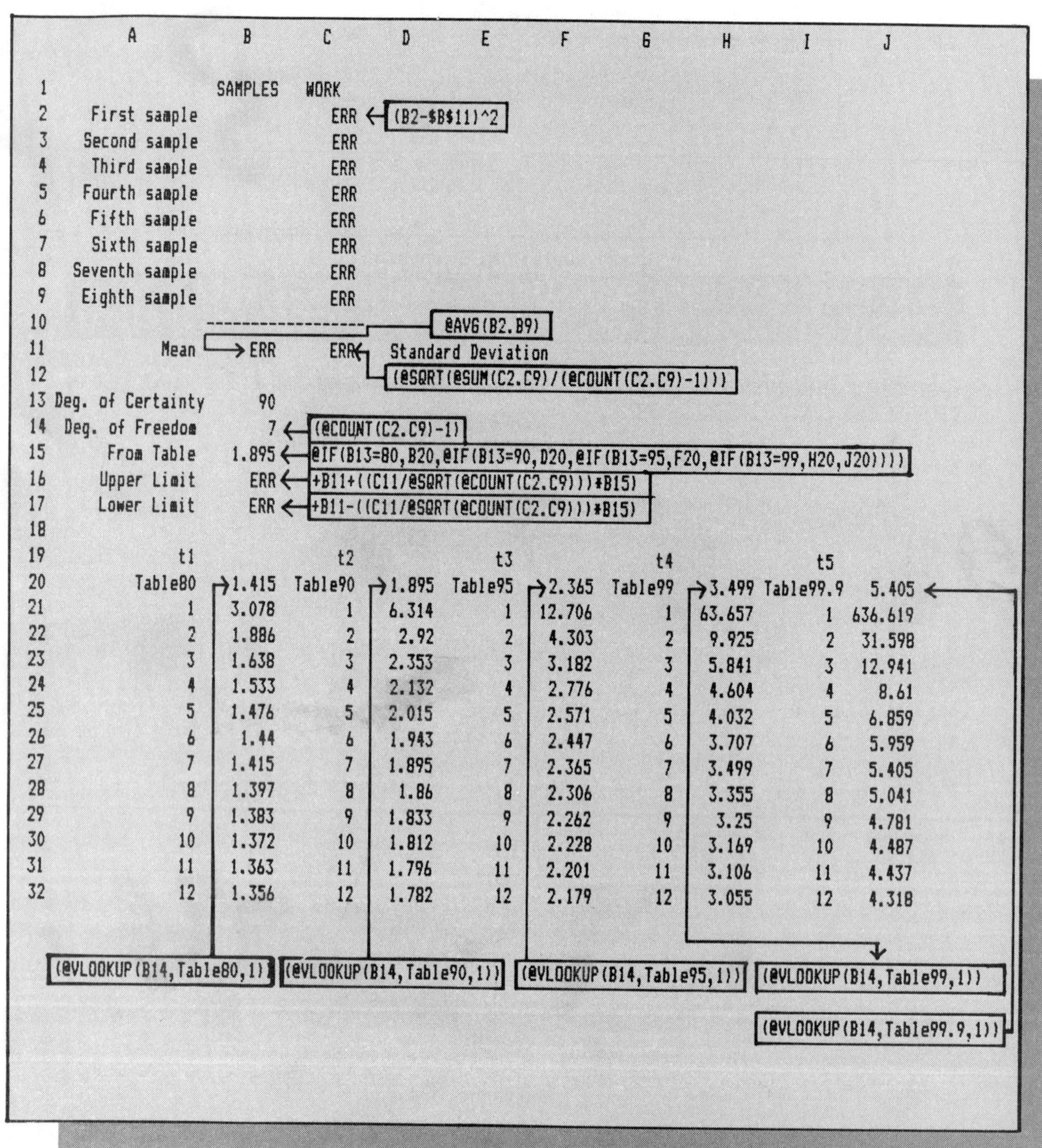

Figure 1

Now type in the labels THROUGH ROW 17 ONLY of your worksheet.

Don't forget to type in the label in A11 (Mean), as well as the label in D11 (Standard Deviation).

Now that you have entered the labels THROUGH ROW 17, you will want to right-justify them. To do this,

Place your cursor on A2 and type:

/R	starts RANGE command
L	selects Label option
R	selects Right option and displays A2

Move your cursor, with the arrow keys, to A17. The screen will reverse to show you the area being right-justified.

RETURN	executes the command

Next you will enter the dashed lines in row 10, columns B and C.

Place your cursor on B10 and type:

\	starts REPEAT command
—	label to be repeated
RETURN	executes the command

Now copy the dashed line over to column C.

Leave your cursor on B10 and type:

/C	starts COPY command and displays B10
RETURN	displays Range to copy to
C10	coordinate to copy to
RETURN	executes the command

TYPING IN THE TABLES AT THE BOTTOM HALF OF YOUR WORKSHEET

USE THE FOLLOWING STEP-BY-STEP DIRECTIONS TO TYPE IN THE TABLES AT THE BOTTOM OF YOUR WORKSHEET:

First type in the labels in ROW 19. To do this,

Place your cursor on A19 and type:

t1   label

[RETURN]   enters the label

Place your cursor on C19 and type:

t2   label

[RETURN]   enters the label

Continue typing in the labels in row 19, into columns E, G and I.

Next you will type in the labels in ROW 20. To do this,

Place your cursor on A20 and type:

Table80   label

[RETURN]   enters the label

Place your cursor on C20 and type:

Table90   label

[RETURN]   enters the label

Continue typing in the labels across ROW 20, into columns E, G and I.

Now you will right-justify the labels in ROWS 19 and 20.

Place your cursor on A19 and type:

/R   starts RANGE command

L   selects Label option

R   selects Right option and displays A19

Move your cursor, with the arrow keys, to I20. The screen will reverse to show you the area being right-justified.

RETURN   executes the command

Now that you have typed in the labels in the tables, you will begin entering the known values.

ENTERING VALUES INTO THE TABLES

USE THE FOLLOWING STEP-BY-STEP DIRECTIONS FOR ENTERING THE KNOWN VALUES INTO THE TABLES:

NOTE

Be careful when entering the values into the tables. DO NOT ENTER any of the values in ROW 20. (Later in the exercise, you will be entering formulas there.)

Start entering your labels on ROW 21, immediately under Table80. To do this,

Place your cursor on A21 and type:

1   value

RETURN   enters the value

Place your cursor on A22 and type:

2   value

RETURN   enters the value

Continue entering the values down column A, under Table80.

Then go to column B and, BEGINNING ON ROW 21, immediately to the right of 1, type the values down the column.

Continue entering the values into columns C, D, E, F, G, H, I and J, making sure you always begin on ROW 21.

Now that you have typed the known values into the tables, you will name them.

NAMING THE TABLES

USE THE FOLLOWING STEP-BY-STEP DIRECTIONS FOR NAMING THE TABLES:

To name Table 80,

Place your cursor on A21 and type:

/R	starts RANGE command
N	selects Name option
C	selects Create option
Table80	name given to table
RETURN	displays Enter Range: A21

Move your cursor, with arrow keys, to B32. The screen will reverse to show the area being named.

RETURN	executes the command

To name Table 90,

Place your cursor on C21 and type:

/R	starts RANGE command
N	selects Name option
C	selects Create option
Table90	name given to table
RETURN	displays Enter Range: C21

Move your cursor, with arrow keys, to D32. The screen will reverse to show the area being named.

RETURN	executes the command

To name Table 95,

Place your cursor on E21 and type:

/R	starts RANGE command
N	selects Name option
C	selects Create option
Table95	name given to table
RETURN	displays Enter Range: E21

Move your cursor, with arrow keys, to F32. The screen will reverse to show the area being named.

| RETURN | executes the command |

To name Table 99,

Place your cursor on G21 and type:

| /R | starts RANGE command |

| N | selects Name option |

| C | selects Create option |

| Table99 | name given to table |

| RETURN | displays Enter Range: G21 |

Move your cursor, with arrow keys, to H32. The screen will reverse to show the area being named.

| RETURN | executes the command |

To name Table 99.9,

Place your cursor on I21 and type:

| /R | starts RANGE command |

| N | selects Namé option |

| C | selects Create option |

| Table99.9 | name given to table |

| RETURN | displays Enter Range: I21 |

Move your cursor, with arrow keys, to J32. The screen will reverse to show the area being named.

| RETURN | executes the command |

ENTERING THE FORMULAS

USE THE FOLLOWING STEP-BY-STEP DIRECTIONS FOR ENTERING THE FORMULAS
WHICH WILL CALCULATE THE UNKNOWN VALUES.

Before entering the formulas, you will FIRST ENTER THE VALUE INTO COORDINATE B13,
which is the Degree of Certainty desired.

Place your cursor on B13 and type:

| 90 | degree of certainty |

| RETURN | enters the value |

Now you are ready to begin entering the formulas.

Formula one, in column B, to the right of **Mean**, calculates the mean for the sampales.

Place your cursor on B11 and type:

@ A V G (B 2 . B 9)   formula

RETURN   enters the formula

Formula two, in column C, immediately under **WORK**, calculates the mean for the first sample.

NOTE

1-2-3 is designed to do one of two things with coordinates when they are copied. The coordinates are either relative to their new location or they remain absolute, which means they remain the same.

A coordinate address is relative unless it is converted to an absolute by having a dollar sign ($) preceding the column designation and/or row designation, i.e. (B11).

A quick way to make a coordinate absolute is by placing your cursor on that coordinate and pressing the F4 key, which will automatically place the dollar as shown.

In formula two, which you are about to enter, the value in B11 must remain absolute when you copy the formula down the column later. You will note that, in order to accomplish this, when you enter the formula you will be typing B11.

To enter formula two,

Place your cursor on C2 and type:

(B 2 — $ B $ 1 1)^2   formula

RETURN   enters the formula

Now you will copy this formula down the **WORK** column to the dashed line.

Leave your cursor on C2 and type:

/C   starts COPY command and displays Range to copy from:
                                         C2

RETURN   displays Range to copy to

C3   first coordinate to copy to

.   ellipsis - indicates from-to

C9   last coordinate to copy to

RETURN   executes the command

Formula three in column C, underneath the dashed line, and to the left of Standard Deviation, calculates the sample standard deviation.

Place your cursor on C11 and type:

(@ S Q R T (@ S U M (C 2 . C 9) / (@ COUNT (C 2 . C 9) — 1)))   formula

RETURN   enters the formula

ENTERING FORMULAS IN THE TABLES

USE THE FOLLOWING STEP-BY-STEP DIRECTIONS FOR ENTERING THE FORMULAS, IN THE TABLES, WHICH WILL CALCULATE THE UNKNOWN VALUES:

You will now enter formulas in ROW 20 of the tables.

Formula four, to the right of Table 80, looks up the degree of freedom in Table 80.

NOTE

In formula four, as well as formulas five, six, seven and eight, which you are about to enter, the LOOKUP function will be used to look up a value in a table.

The table in this exercise is in a column format, which means that it is in a Vertical format. Therefore, the LOOKUP function being used will be indicated by @VLOOKUP. (The V indicates that the table is in Vertical, or column, format.)

The left-most column of the table is considered the labels of the table, and the adjacent column to the right contains the values. This adjacent column to the right is called the first offset. In the formulas which you are about to enter, the 1 after the table name, refers to this first offset. (Example: Table80,1)

If the table were in a row format, or a Horizontal format, the LOOKUP function being used would be indicated by @HLOOKUP, the H indicating that the table is in Horizontal, or row format. Then the top-most row would be considered the labels of the table, and row beneath it would contain the values, and would be called the first offset.

To enter formula four,

Place your cursor on B20 and type:

(@ VLOOKUP (B 1 4 , Table80 , 1))   formula

RETURN   enters the formula

Formula five, to the right of Table 90, looks up the degree of freedom in Table 90.

Place your cursor on D20 and type:

(@ VLOOKUP (B 1 4 , Table90 , 1))   formula

RETURN   enters the formula

Formula six, to the right of Table95, looks up the degree of freedom in Table 95.

Place your cursor on F20 and type:

(@ VLOOKUP (B 1 4 , Table95 , 1))   formula

RETURN   enters the formula

Formula seven, to the right of Table99, looks up the degree of freedom in Table 99.

Place your cursor on H20 and type:

(@ VLOOKUP (B 1 4 , Table99 , 1))   formula

RETURN   enters the formula

Formula eight, to the right of Table99.9, looks up the degree of freedom in Table 99.9.

Place your cursor on J20 and type:

(@ VLOOKUP (B 1 4 , Table99.9 , 1))   formula

RETURN   enters the formula

ENTERING THE FORMULAS IN THE UPPER HALF OF YOUR WORKSHEET

USE THE FOLLOWING STEP-BY-STEP DIRECTIONS FOR ENTERING THE FORMULAS, IN THE UPPER HALF OF YOUR WORKSHEET, WHICH WILL CALCULATE THE UNKNOWN VALUES.

Return to the upper half of your worksheet and enter the following formulas:

Formula nine, in column B, to the right of Degree of Freedom, represents the degrees of freedom desired.

Place your cursor on B14 and type:

(@ COUNT (C 2 . C 9) — 1)   formula

RETURN   enters the formula

Formula ten in column B, to the right of From Table, is the appropriate value selected from the Tables, depending on the degree of certainty desired. (In this exercise, 90 is the degree of certainty desired.)

Place your cursor on B15 and type:

@IF (B13 = 80,B20,@IF (B13 = 90,D20,@IF (B13 = 95,F20,@IF (B13 = 99,H20,J20)))) formula

RETURN   enters the formula

Formula eleven, in column B, to the right of Upper Limit of additives allowed in the fruit juice.

Place your cursor on B16 and type:

+ B11 + ((C11 / @SQRT (@COUNT (C2.C9))) * B15)   formula

RETURN   enters the formula

Formula twelve, in column B, to the right of Lower Limit, calculates the allowable lower limit of additives allowed in the fruit juice.

Place your cursor on B17 and type:

+ B11 — ((C11 / @SQRT (@COUNT (C2.C9))) * B15)   formula

RETURN   enters the formula

Now you will format the coordinates into which you have just entered formulas 11 and 12, so that they will be dispalyed with two decimal places.

Place your cursor on B16 and type:

/R	starts RANGE command
F	selects Format option
F	selects Fixed option and displays number of decimal places: 2
RETURN	displays Range to format: B16

Move your cursor, with arrow keys, to B17. Screen will reverse to show which coordinates are being formatted.

RETURN	executes the command

Your worksheet should now look like Figure 1.

MAKING WORKSHEET ENTRIES

NOTE

Never enter values into coordinates containing formulas, or the formulas will be erased.

USING THE FOLLOWING DIRECTIONS, make your worksheet entries, as illustrated in Figure 2.

	A	B	C	D	E	F	G	H	I	J
1		SAMPLES	WORK							
2	First sample	15.2	0.2025							
3	Second sample	15	0.4225							
4	Third sample	15.7	0.0025							
5	Fourth sample	15.9	0.0625							
6	Fifth sample	15.8	0.0225							
7	Sixth sample	16.1	0.2025							
8	Seventh sample	15.6	0.0025							
9	Eighth sample	15.9	0.0625							
10		------------------								
11	Mean	15.65	0.37	Standard Deviation						
12										
13	Deg. of Certainty	90								
14	Deg. of Freedom	7								
15	From Table	1.895								
16	Upper Limit	15.90								
17	Lower Limit	15.40								
18										
19	t1		t2		t3		t4		t5	
20	Table80	1.415	Table90	1.895	Table95	2.365	Table99	3.499	Table99.9	5.405
21	1	3.078	1	6.314	1	12.706	1	63.657	1	636.619
22	2	1.886	2	2.92	2	4.303	2	9.925	2	31.598
23	3	1.638	3	2.353	3	3.182	3	5.841	3	12.941
24	4	1.533	4	2.132	4	2.776	4	4.604	4	8.61
25	5	1.476	5	2.015	5	2.571	5	4.032	5	6.859
26	6	1.44	6	1.943	6	2.447	6	3.707	6	5.959
27	7	1.415	7	1.895	7	2.365	7	3.499	7	5.405
28	8	1.397	8	1.86	8	2.306	8	3.355	8	5.041
29	9	1.383	9	1.833	9	2.262	9	3.25	9	4.781
30	10	1.372	10	1.812	10	2.228	10	3.169	10	4.487
31	11	1.363	11	1.796	11	2.201	11	3.106	11	4.437
32	12	1.356	12	1.782	12	2.179	12	3.055	12	4.318

Figure 2

Place your cursor on B2, immediately to the right of First Sample, and type:

15.2	value

RETURN	enters the value

Now continue typing in the values down the column until you reach the dashed line.

Last, format coordinate C11 to read as two decimal places.

Place your cursor on C11 and type:

/R	starts RANGE command
F	selects Format option
F	selects Fixed option and displays number of decimal places: 2

RETURN	displays Range to format: C11

RETURN	executes the command

Now your worksheet should look like Figure 2.

Now that your worksheet is complete, it is ready and all you need to do is enter your own set of known values.

SAVING YOUR WORKSHEET

Now save your worksheet for future use, so that the next time you wish to figure these computations all you will need to do is enter in your new known values, and you will not need to retype in the labels or enter the formulas.

To save your worksheet, place a formatted data diskette in Drive A.

With your cursor on any location, type:

/F	starts FILE command
S	selects Save option

Type in name of file.

RETURN	executes the command

PRINTING YOUR WORKSHEET

To print all or a portion of your worksheet, use the following directions, which are given for the Epson printer (compressed font).

Place your cursor on A1 and type:

/P	starts PRINT command
P	displays options
O	selects Options option
S	Selects Setup option and displays: Enter Setup String
\ 015	sets an Epson printer to compressed font
RETURN	accepts setup and displays options
M	selects Margin option
R	selects Right option
230	characters per line
RETURN	displays options
Q	selects Quit option and returns to main print menu
R	displays Range to print from
.	ellipsis - indicates from-to

Move cursor, with arrow keys, to last coordinate in area you wish to print. The screen will reverse to indicate the area being printed.

RETURN	executes the command
G	selects Go option and prints

To exit out of PRINT command, type:

Q	selects Quit option and exits out of PRINT command

LOADING YOUR WORKSHEET BACK INTO LOTUS 1-2-3

At a later date, when you need to use the worksheet to do further computations, just load your worksheet back into memory.

To do this, you must first clear memory if there is anything in it. To clear the memory,

Leave your cursor on any location and type:

/W	starts WORKSHEET command
E	selects Erase option
Y	Yes, to confirm

Now you are ready to load the worksheet into the memory, using 1-2-3's FILE command. To do this,

Place the data diskette from which you wish to load into Drive A.

Leave your cursor on any location and type:

/F	starts FILE command
R	selects Retrieve option

Place your cursor on the file name you wish to load, and press:

RETURN	executes the command

INDEX OF FUNCTIONS AND COMMANDS

(continued on next page)

REPEAT

WORKSHEET

Note: Some of the above functions and commands appear in more pages than listed in this
index.

REFERENCES

Farish and Breynolds, et al, <u>Calculator Analysis for Business and Finance</u>

Grawoig, Fielitz, Robinson, and Tabor, <u>Mathematics: A Foundation for Decisions</u>

Greynolds, et al, <u>Executive Calculator Guidebook</u>

Horngren, <u>Cost Accounting: A Managerial Emphasis</u>

Kieso and Weygandt, <u>Intermediate Accounting</u>

Miller and Orr, <u>A Model of the Demand for Money by Firms</u>

Weston and Brigham, <u>Essentials of Managerial Finance</u>

NOTES

NOTES

NOTES

NOTES